DREAMS AND INNER JOURNEYS

MYSTERIES LIBRARY:

DREAMS AND INNER JOURNEYS

EXPLORING SPIRITUAL AND SHAMANIC RITUALS FOR SELF-AWARENESS AND PERSONAL DISCOVERY

WILL ADCOCK

ROSALIND POWELL * LAURA J WATTS

LORENZ BOOKS

This edition is published by Lorenz Books

Lorenz Books is an imprint of Anness Publishing Ltd
Hermes House, 88–89 Blackfriars Road, London SE1 8HA
tel. 020 7401 2077; fax 020 7633 9499
www.lorenzbooks.com; info@anness.com

UK agent: The Manning Partnership Ltd, 6 The Old Dairy, Melcombe Road, Bath BA2 3LR
tel. 01225 478444; fax 01225 478440; sales@manning-partnership.co.uk

UK distributor: Grantham Book Services Ltd, Isaac Newton Way, Alma Park Industrial Estate, Grantham
Lincs NG31 9SD; tel. 01476 541080; fax 01476 541061; orders@gbs.tbs-ltd.co.uk

North American agent/distributor: National Book Network, 4501 Forbes Boulevard, Suite 200, Lanham
MD 20706; tel. 301 459 3366; fax 301 429 5746; www.nbnbooks.com

Australian agent/distributor: Pan Macmillan Australia, Level 18, St Martins Tower, 31 Market St, Sydney
NSW 2000; tel. 1300 135 113; fax 1300 135 103; customer.service@macmillan.com.au

New Zealand agent/distributor: David Bateman Ltd, 30 Tarndale Grove, Off Bush Road, Albany, Auckland
tel. (09) 415 7664; fax (09) 415 8892

Publisher: Joanna Lorenz
Managing Editor: Helen Sudell
Project Editors: Emma Gray and Debra Mayhew
Designer: Axis Design
Photographer: Don Last
Production Controller: Claire Rae
Illustrators: Garry Walton and Robert Highton
Editorial Reader: Joy Wotton

Previously published as *Dream Wisdom and Shamanism*

1 3 5 7 9 10 8 6 4 2

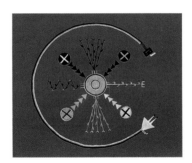

contents

introduction

The spiritual web of life on earth binds together an amalgamation of human beings, animals, plants, rocks and water. All are fundamentally linked by energy. It suffuses all things, and each part of creation vibrates at its own particular frequency and has its own natural rhythm; which means it harmonizes with all other things. By allowing yourself to become more receptive to this all-enveloping spirit, you can tune in to the earth's secret energy, reaching new depths of insight and understanding that will help you find your own place in the great pattern of creation and achieve your true life's goals.

journeying to other worlds

The wise ones of old were shamans: healers and medicine men, witch doctors and diviners. They were often born with the seed of knowing, choosing to be chosen by the magical world, and frequently going through such intense personal experiences as illness or trauma before their gifts were revealed to them. In most cases they were simple people, living simple lives. What set them apart was their awareness that ancient wisdom lay within the self.

To be a true shaman is to walk between worlds, having no fear of death or darkness, understanding this to be the other side of life and light. The shaman works with energy, with natural forces as well as nature herself, and understands that the physical world is not the only reality. Other worlds, such as the dreamworld we inhabit each night while we sleep, have equal validity for the shaman, who journeys to other realms of creation with the conscious intention of communicating with spirits and gaining wisdom and insights that can be brought back to the physical world. Acting as an intermediary, the shaman will seek the help of "good spirits" (or vital energies) and will negotiate with "bad spirits" (or dense energies) to

return a sick person to health or to help someone acting out of character back to their happier self. The shaman is the spiritual warrior, who faces life's challenges with courage and daring.

In the modern world, the techniques that were evolved by traditional shamans to heighten their consciousness can be used to explore and discover your own place in the universe. By following their path, you can come to see more clearly how you are enmeshed in the whole of creation. Shamanism allows you to connect with the energy that flows throughout the universe, so that you begin to sense the vibration of other life forms and to discern different realms of existence. These new insights can help you to a greater understanding of your place in the universe and, hence, your own nature.

growth   wisdom
nner peace

This book provides a clear and simple introduction to some traditional shamanic techniques: these simple and direct expressions of intent will help you to create a space in which your intuition can flourish. Working on visualizations will allow you to create your own personal sacred space, a safe and secure place to which you can return again and again for spiritual nourishment, and which can form the starting point for shamanic journeying and dreamwork.

The traditional tools of the shaman can be used to focus your intent and express reverence and respect for the natural environment: the burning of purifying herbs and incense is sanctifying and cleansing, and can be used in simple rituals on yourself, on other people and on places that are important to you. Making an offering on a personal altar or in a place that is special to you is another ritual act that helps to signify your conscious intent and helps you to connect with nature.

Shamans traditionally performed repetitive, rhythmic dances and chants to heighten their state of awareness, beating drums to sustain and underline the rhythm of their movements. A regular drumbeat is a useful aid to spiritual journeying – if you have no one to drum for you while you go on your journey, you can bring this traditional practice into the modern world by making a recording of your own drumming.

Shamanic practices help to develop a deeper relationship with all life, including your own inner world. There is nothing to fear, because at the heart of you is a beautiful being of light. Your journey will be taking you only through the darkness of your own ignorance to the wise one that waits within.

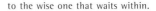

Dreams hold the key to understanding the world of subconscious fears, hopes and ideals. They can also reveal areas of your life that require your attention, asking you to heal unresolved issues. Out of the darkest recesses of your being, your dreams can reveal far more than you ever imagined, if you are prepared to spend the time reaching an understanding of their message.

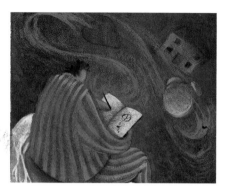

About a quarter of the time you are asleep is taken up with dreams – approximately two hours a night. The importance of dreaming to mental and emotional wellbeing is still being investigated, but it has been found that people who are experimentally deprived of dreaming sleep quickly become irritable and distracted, and need to dream more frequently than normal as soon as they are allowed to sleep again. The dreams you remember most clearly when you wake tend to be those that have deep personal significance. In many cases you may remember only a few confused and fleeting images, but some dreams are vivid, and will repay detailed analysis, perhaps leading you to re-assess aspects of your life and surprising you with what they reveal about your inner world.

If you can practise lucid dreaming, you can work with a dream while you are experiencing it, questioning whoever appears in it in order to draw out its meaning. It is possible to develop the ability to dream lucidly, using techniques that make you aware that you are dreaming. Dream incubation is another technique for controlling your dreams, helping you to choose subjects to dream before you go to sleep.

Keeping a dream diary will help you to analyse dreams of particular significance to you. The dominant motifs in your dreams may be hard to interpret, and all symbols will have a meaning that is specific to your own personal circumstances, but the interpretations given in this book may help by acting as starting points for your own ideas.

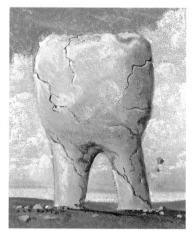

One way to achieve a greater understanding of your inner world is to develop a deeper relationship with patterns and symbols, not only in dreams but in the external world. A traditional shamanic symbol is the circular medicine wheel or sacred hoop, which is divided into four sections representing the seasons and the cardinal points. It is used as a focus for meditation. Mandalas are similar visual tools. The powerful image of the wheel is used in the ceremonies and rituals of many cultures, from the Hindu Yantra to the Celtic Cross and the Navajo Blessingway. Some of these traditional patterns are

dreamworld symbols

inner world truth

described here in detail so that you can reproduce them for yourself, or use them as inspiration for the creation of your own personal mandala.

The Tibetan Wheel of Time is a two-dimensional representation of the universe, representing the true, three-dimensional Buddhist mandala, which exists only in the mind's eye. Tibetan monks create the intricate patterns of the Wheel of Time by pouring coloured sand on to a sanctified circle on the floor, in a ceremony which brings healing to its surroundings. Once the design is finished, its healing power is released as the sand is swept up from the floor and returned to the natural world.

Meditation on the mandala can lead you to an appreciation of the symmetry of nature, and to see that the world itself is one huge mandala: a vast pattern for contemplation, of which you are a part. From this source, you can begin to find your own patterns. Whether you gaze up at the circling stars in the night sky, or look into the intricate symmetry of a snowflake, the order of the universe is apparent all around you.

You can also create new patterns that reflect who you would like to be as you journey through life. Form your own mandalas to explore your inner being, drawing on the significance of colour, shape and numbers to elucidate your chosen path. This book includes guidance for meditation and explains how you can use mandala meditation to achieve inner wholeness and harmony, and to bring healing changes in times of stress and conflict. To meditate upon geometric shapes, patterns or symbols can be a very powerful experience of an unspoken language. In the modern period, the potency of the circle as a means of self-expression was explored by the psychologist C. G. Jung, who saw the

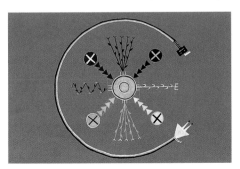

mandala as a representation of the psyche, with the true self of the individual at its centre.

Walking the wheel of life with an open heart and a willingness to learn will bring an undreamt-of richness into your world. The ways of ancient wisdom are available to anyone who steps out to claim them. You can choose to be chosen – all you have to do is take the first step.

shamanism

shamanism
shamanism

Shamanism is essentially a state of mind, a way of viewing life as a whole. The shaman gains insights and wisdom by connecting with other parts of creation and sets out to heal the divisions that exist between its separate pieces. Such divisions can occur anywhere: within the self, within groups of people, between human beings and the environment, and so on.

The word "shaman" comes from the Tungusic dialect of the Ural-Altaic tribes of Siberia. Shamans were the priest-doctors of the tribes, responsible for officiating at ceremonies and rituals, advising the elders, tending the sick and injured and caring for the spiritual well-being of the people. More recently, the term has become a more or less generic word, used in reference to anyone who fulfils that role in traditional societies all around the world.

Shamanism does not recognize differences of age, gender, race or religious doctrines and so is available to all. Indeed, many people have had shamanic experiences without labelling them as such. Like everything else on earth, human beings are part of creation, and shamanism is the human way of connecting with the whole. It is a fundamental part of our heritage and, although the connection may be weakened by the pressures of modern life, the ability to connect and the inclination to do so is still present. This introduction to shamanic practice will guide you towards wisdom and insight through the use of rituals, spiritual journeying and working with dreams.

tradition and spirit

When communities were much more isolated and self-reliant than modern society, shamans played an integral part in their cultures. They treated the sick and injured, but they were not specifically healers. Although they communed with ancestors, spirits and gods, they were not priests, and while they offered counsel to their communities, they were not solely sages. Rather, they fulfilled a combination of these roles.

The Shaman's Role

To understand the function of a shaman, it is necessary to adopt a world view relative to traditional peoples. Typically, older cultures more in touch with the natural world have been animistic societies. Animism is a term derived from the Latin *anima*, which means soul, and these older cultures held the belief that all things possessed a soul or spirit. The fundamental role of the shaman was to act as an intermediary in relating to the other spirits of the earth: the animals, the land, the rain, the crops and so on. Because humans were so dependent on the forces of nature and the other beings of the planet, communicating with them was seen as a way of predicting problems or finding a way out of them. The

Wearing animal skins helped a shaman commune with the spirits.

shaman could send his or her soul out on a journey to meet with these other spirits, and ensure a successful hunt or determine why a crop was failing, or if there would be a drought. These journeys of the soul could also lead shamans to other dimensions where they would commune with gods, find special knowledge or acquire powers.

It was this ability to travel to other realms that marked out the shaman. Often it was unlooked for, with visions occurring spontaneously, or caused by traumatic experiences. What is often now termed "madness" was seen as being "touched by the gods". Shamans usually lived apart from the community, but individuals who could hear voices and experience realities beyond normal perception were regarded with respect. Altered states of consciousness could be induced by a shaman seeking to go on a journey. The drum was a very powerful shamanic tool, seen as a mode of transporting the soul on its regular beat as it opened gateways for the shaman. Dancing was another method employed to achieve a trance state, usually to contact a specific animal spirit. By moving the body in a way that mimicked the animal in question, the shaman became that animal and was able to relate directly to it. Costume was also important in this respect and the use of feathers, skins, bones and significant designs was seen as a way of linking with spirits and journeying to other dimensions.

Sacred plants have long been used as a means of accessing spirit worlds. In Europe, fly agaric, psilocybe mushrooms and doses of hemlock were all used as vehicles by which a shaman could enter an altered state of consciousness. In Mexico, the peyote cactus was, and still is, eaten to bring the shaman into contact with the spirit of the universe. Such plants induce visionary trances and heightened telepathic abilities which allow the shaman to "tune in" to the different levels of creation or travel to otherworlds. Because of the powers of these sacred plants, they need to be approached with respect and ceremony.

Traditional shamans, then, held a position of influence but also one of great responsibility. The people would turn to them first in matters of importance, and the shamans would use their abilities and powers to find a satisfactory outcome.

A North American Blackfoot shaman in ceremonial robes.

Merlin dictates his history to a scribe.

Legendary Shamans

In the European cultures there are many myths of shamans and shamanic adventures. Ceridwen was a great Celtic shaman who brewed a magic potion to confer infinite knowledge on her son, but the kitchen boy drank it and acquired all her wisdom. During a shapeshifting chase to catch him, she became a hen and he a grain of corn. Ceridwen ate the corn and became pregnant with the Celtic bard, Taliesin. In the Arthurian legends, Merlin possessed divinatory powers and could shapeshift, commune with animals and spirits and travel to the otherworlds.

Odin, the chief god of the Scandinavian Pantheon, was another famous shaman. He gave up one of his eyes in return for a drink from the well of Mimir, the source of all wisdom. He also sacrificed himself on the World Tree to learn the wisdom of the dead, bringing back runes from the underworld.

Modern Shamanism

Traditional shamanism still exists in many places in the world, especially where the old cultures remain strong. It is not uncommon for people to seek the assistance of a shaman in the lands of the Arctic, Africa, Australasia, Indonesia, North and South America, Mongolia, China and Tibet. Although in modern Western societies there seems to be little need for a shaman to help with problems about food, the weather or disgruntled gods, there is a place for shamanism on a personal level. Shamanism is a way to find our place in the universe. By embarking upon a shamanic journey to other levels of consciousness, the modern shaman can reach depths of insight that can lead to enlightenment.

Connecting with Spirit

What is spirit? How can it be defined? Spirit is the omnipresent energy possessed by all things. It is the essence of creation, the unifying force that is present throughout the universe. Spirit connects us one with another, but also with animals, plants, rocks, water, air, the stars and the space between the stars. It is the skein of being beyond the physical that can be accessed for communication, for healing and for understanding.

Imagine a spider's web, a beautifully delicate construction designed to catch flies and transmit vibrations. The structure is continuous, so that the whole is affected to some degree wherever an insect is trapped in it. Moreover, the spider can differentiate between the struggling of a trapped fly and the vibration set up by, say, the wind or an airborne seed. The simile of a web is used in many traditional societies to illustrate the principle of connectedness, and the same analogy is used in the modern world – in the World Wide Web, the information superhighway, which permits worldwide communication in virtually no time at all. Just think of the energy incorporated here – energy that is an extension of the universal energy, the spirit of creation.

All of us are aware of energy on an instinctive level. We have all experienced atmospheres; in a room after an argument has occurred so much energy has been emitted that the air is thick with it. On a more subtle level, there is the instinctive feeling that you are liked or disliked by someone. Because humans have closely linked vibrations, the energy is readily sensed by other humans. A shaman can extend this sensitivity to feel the vibrations of other parts of creation.

Energy is apparent all around us.

sacred space

Do you have a place that you find especially conducive to meditation or relaxation? Perhaps a tree in a park or in your garden, a certain rock outcrop or a wood where you often walk. Anywhere that you feel comfortable can be a sacred space, and that can include a place within yourself: sometimes it's not possible to travel physically to a special place to unwind just when you need to, so why not carry it with you?

Sacred Sites

There are many examples of sacred sites around the world that have special significance to particular societies: Stonehenge for the Druids; Mount Olympus for the Greeks; the San Francisco Mountains for the native American Zuni tribe; the Black Hills of South Dakota for the plains tribes; and Uluru (formerly known as Ayers Rock) for the Australian tribes. These sites are usually powerful places associated with the ancestors, gods or spirits of a given culture. Their power has been augmented by the accumulated energy of many generations who have assembled there for sacred rites or meditation, and over time they have become increasingly important to the collective psyche of the society. Sacred space approaches the concept on a more personal level.

Your sacred space is a safe, secure place.

Your Own Sacred Space

The inner sacred space is a place that you can create inside yourself. You can use this special place as a sanctuary, a retreat from the outside world, where you can relax and recoup your spiritual energies. The place you create can resemble anything in the physical world that makes you feel comfortable: a desert island, a hut on a mountain, a cave, anything. Maybe it's a place that you already know; somewhere you have visited before, either in a dream or in this world. The more you visualize your sacred space, the more real it will seem, so try to feel textures, see details, hear sounds and smell scents.

Your sacred space is a safe place and, because it is always there, you can visit it at any time. It can evolve as much as you want it to, because you created it and the control over it lies only with you. The only limitations on it are ones that you, as the maker, impose yourself. So, be aware of what comes into being in your visualization, for that can offer important insights into your subconscious. This private place is a good jumping-off point for beginning journeys.

Experiencing Nature

The natural world is a great place to find peace, tranquillity and inspiration, and to practise visualizing details to put into your own sacred space. Get out and walk in beautiful, wild places as much as possible to experience the benefits that a natural environment can bring. When you are out walking, be receptive and aware of your surroundings: admire the beauty of a tree, a flower or a bird in flight and always be grateful. Remember that life is a precious gift to be appreciated now.

Nature can give us many things to help remind us of our connection. While you are out walking you may find stones, feathers, sticks, intricate patterns and images, but if anything is taken, remember to leave something else in return as an offering, an exchange of energy to signify your appreciation of the gift that has been given to you. Shamanism is about relating to the natural world and your place in it.

Take time to stop, relax and meditate on the incredible complexity of the creation around you. To help your meditation, close your eyes and see how much sharper your other senses become. Extend that receptivity to feel the land, and blend with it. Feel what is around you: the vitality of the earth, the immensity of the world and the universe beyond. You are a part of it, be aware and accept the experience for what it is: humbling and precious.

Visualizing Sacred Space

Before you begin journeying or dreamwork you need to work on visualizing a place in your mind that becomes your own personal sacred space. The sacred space you create will be your place and only people you invite may enter. It can be any kind of place in which your spirit feels happy and at home: a woodland clearing, a cave, a deserted beach, even a corner of your own garden. The more times you visit your sacred space the more real it will seem and the easier it will be to get there. Concentrate on creating and remembering detail; love the place, care for it, plant flowers and trees and tend them as they grow, decorate it as you would your home. Work out rituals for arriving and leaving and, from time to time, imagine making an offering there to help express your gratitude.

Expanding the Visualization

Now picture an opening: a natural doorway such as a hole in the ground or the mouth of a cave. This will lead you to the sacred space you seek. When you pass through, pay attention to details that will make the place seem more real. Utilize all your senses to give the place solidity. This is tricky to achieve at first, but with a little practice it will get easier.

Expand your senses. Touch trees and feel the texture of the bark; sit on a rock and feel its surface – is it smooth or rough? Feel the warmth of the sun as you walk through the place. What is beneath your feet? Grass, sand, a path? Pause to smell the delicate fragrance of a flower, the bloom redolent with its essence of attraction. Look into it and notice how bright the colours are and how the petals and stamens are arranged. Hear the birdsong and the sighing of the wind. Sit down by a stream, taste the

Use all your senses to make the place as real as possible.

refreshing coolness of the water and absorb the beauty and peace around you.

When you feel it is time to leave, give thanks and promise to return. Retrace your steps through the entrance, back into your physical body. Come slowly back to this world.

Entering Sacred Space

Use these simple steps to begin to build and enter your own inner sacred space. As with all shamanic practices, it is good to concentrate on achieving a calm, grounded and open state of mind before you begin. Breathe slowly and deeply from your diaphragm and use your breathing to help you release any worries that are distracting you.

When you feel relaxed, picture your spirit body stepping out of your physical body. Your spirit body is beautiful, glowing, solid and real, connected to your earthly body by a thin filament. Look down at yourself, sitting or lying peacefully, before you start the journey.

Develop a ritual that feels right for you, and repeat the same steps whenever you enter your sacred space at the beginning of future journeys. Practise a similar ritual for returning to this world.

1 Take five deep breaths to centre yourself and focus on what you are about to do. Voice your intent out loud. Light a candle and burn some incense, holding your intention in your mind.

2 Contemplate the candle flame quietly for a while. As you watch it, imagine that it is lighting up the recesses inside you so that you may find a way to the place you seek more easily.

altars

We're all familiar with altars, and the term probably conjures up some richly decorated object that is the focus of attention in a temple or church. A small personal altar, made using a natural object such as a stone or a log, can be placed in your home or garden and will serve the same purpose for you. It needn't be showy, although bright colours have a greater impact on the subconscious, and therefore a greater power.

Natural Altars

You may come across a special place when out walking, such as a tree or a rock, which you can use as a temporary altar on which to leave an offering to celebrate that particular moment in time. Being in a more public place, a natural altar also has the advantage that others might see it too, and add their energy to the place.

Trees make very beautiful natural altars, pleasing to the eye and very calming when attention is focused upon them. Being firmly rooted, a tree has a deep connection with Mother Earth and that energy can be tapped

Natural altars can show appreciation for the moment.

into when you talk to it, leave offerings and pray or meditate there. You can tie things in the branches for decoration, or place tiny items in the trunk. A flat rock placed at the base of the trunk can serve as an altarstone. Be aware of which trees attract you, because they all have their own attributes and symbolism. For example, oak is the keeper of wisdom and possesses great strength; willow represents love and regeneration because it is able to grow a new tree from a cut branch; the very tall and

graceful beech symbolizes aspirations to higher ideals; yew, associated with ancient burial sites, represents transformation and inner wisdom.

Rocks are the bones of the Mother, supporting her and therefore us. Because they take millions of years to form, they hold within them a rich store of ancient earth wisdom and knowledge, power and strength. They aid in connecting with the earth because they are so much a part of it, being formed deep within. Call upon this strength when you pray at a rock altar and feel it helping you, supporting you and connecting you.

Indoor Altars

An altar in your home can be made using a flat rock or a piece of wood or a small table. Whatever you use, look after it, keep it clean and give it your attention for a few minutes each day. The altar will help to focus your awareness and strengthen your spiritual connections.

Making a Cairn

The beauty of making something to use as an altar is that the maker's energy is blended with the materials in a focused way. A cairn serves very well as a natural altar. It can look like a haphazard pile of stones but, to make it stable, care must be taken in selecting stones that fit together well. Take your time as you gather the stones and lay them in position.

1 Begin by selecting a few large, flat, roughly circular rocks to act as the base.

2 Build up a tapering dome by laying smaller flat rocks in an overlapping pattern.

3 As you work, keep the intent of honouring creation, to help focus your energy.

4 When the cairn is complete, decorate it with objects found close by.

Stone Circles

There are many examples of these ancient structures, especially in the British Isles and other parts of Northern Europe. The full purposes for their construction are unclear, although they are accurate astronomical calendars in which certain stones align with celestial bodies at significant times of the year, such as the summer and winter solstices. In North America there are large circles, outlined in stone, at a number of sites. These wheels are orientated to the compass and constructed on sacred sites where people still come to pray and leave offerings.

The intent behind ancient stone circles is obscure, but they have a simple, awe-inspiring majesty such as this one at Castlerigg, Cumbria, England.

Blessing the Stones

The east is the place of illumination, the place of conception. It is the direction represented by spring with all its vigorous new growth. Call on this energy as you bless the stone and place it in the east position.

The south is the place of consolidation, the place of the child. It is the direction represented by summer when the burgeoning life progresses into fullness. Call on this energy as you bless the stone and place it in the south position.

The west is the place of fruition, the place of the adult. It is associated with autumn when the growth reaches its ripeness. Call on this energy as you bless the stone and place it in the west position.

The north is the place of calm reflection, the place of the elder. It is represented by winter, the season when the strength is drawn in. When the growth cycle is past, the elder has the wisdom of experience to reflect upon. Call upon this energy as you bless the stone and place it in the north position.

The stone for Mother Earth is to honour her and thank her for the gifts she gives, the food and shelter she provides, the air she breathes into us and the water that supports us. Recognize her and give thanks as you bless the stone and place it in the circle at the 11 o'clock position, near the centre.

The stone for the spirit is to honour and give thanks for all of creation of which we humans are a part. Recognize the bond as you bless the stone and place it in the circle at the one o'clock position, near the centre.

The stone for the self is to acknowledge the individual's part in the whole and to give thanks for all the things that come to you. Honour the connection as you bless the stone and place it in the circle at the six o'clock position, near the centre.

Making a Stone Circle

Create a sacred space to honour the circle of life and your place in it with your own stone circle. Select seven stones, one each for the four directions, one for Mother Earth, one for the spirit and one for the self.

1 Bless and place the direction stones first, beginning with the one in the east. Each of the directions has its own symbolism and energy.

2 Bless each stone before you lay it in place. Put the three remaining stones inside the circle formed by the four direction stones.

3 The completed stone circle can be used as an altar: as a place to pray, and to give thanks and gain insights into the progression of your life-path.

using herbs and incense

When performing shamanic practices, it is good to begin by preparing yourself spiritually and physically to approach the undertaking in an open and honest manner. Purifying is a very positive act, which both cleanses the spirit and relaxes the body. In many cultures, herbs or incense are burnt for this purpose, the scent acting at a physical level while the smoke washes negative influences from the spirit.

PURIFYING HERBS

Native Americans use several herbs in purifying ceremonies, notably sage, sweetgrass and cedar, either separately or together.

Sage

The term "sage" is a catch-all for the main herbs used in spiritual cleansing. Many varieties of sage and sage-like plants are used, including White Mountain sage, which grows mainly in California, and the sagebrushes and worm-woods, which also favour dry conditions but are found more widely. Sage has a transformative property, working upon negative energies that are somehow clouding an aura. It changes these negative influences to enable them to act for the benefit of the person, place or object whose aura is being cleansed.

Cedar

A purifying incense, cedar is very beneficial for healing on both physical and spiritual levels. The small, flat leaves can be burned alone on a hot rock – as in a sweatlodge – or on a hot coal, or they can be mixed with loose sage into a ball for burning. The

Burning white sage transforms negative energies.

sharp, sweet smoke produced is very refreshing and calming, having an uplifting effect on the spirit and enhancing clarity of mind.

Sweetgrass

Also called "Hair of the Mother", sweetgrass is a tough, fibrous plant that grows in wetland conditions. It is often used to make braids, and attracts beneficial energies to the user, calling on spirits to give strength and guidance.

INCENSE

Burning a joss-stick is a familiar use of incense: you may be in the habit of lighting one simply for its pleasing effect, but when the burning is performed with conscious intent the effect is magnified.

There are many different incenses to choose, with different aromas and properties. Frankincense has been prized for thousands of years. It is a natural tree resin which is often used as a meditation aid. Piñon is a tree resin from North America with cleansing and clarifying properties. Temple Balls are a blend of gums, herbs and oils including elemi, juniper and sandalwood. They cleanse the air, affect atmospheres and relax the body.

Making Sweetgrass Braids

Bundles of sweetgrass are plaited into long braids, which produce a sweet-smelling smoke when burned. Where sage works upon influences that are already present in a person, sweetgrass has the effect of attracting new energy. Native American shamans use sweetgrass in their sweatlodges, where it is rubbed on the red-hot stones to get it smouldering, to invite spiritual allies to join the ceremony. Sweetgrass braids can be bought from alternative and New Age stores, but making your own braid gives greater significance to its burning. Waft the braid in front of your face to inhale the smoke, and repeat four times.

1 Tie up one end of the bundle of sweetgrass, divide into three equal sections and braid.

2 Once the sweetgrass braid is lit, extinguish the flame so that the grass smoulders for a short while.

smudging

When you are smudging, you are cleansing the aura, the energy shell of a physical body. Your aura can become dirty, just like your body. You can wash your body to clean it and you can do the same for your aura. Smudging can be performed on places and objects as well as on people. Visualization, altars and smudging are all ways of creating a sacred space, within and without, and are powerful aids in aligning with universal forces.

Smudge Sticks

Smudge sticks are densely packed bundles of herbs, often including mixtures of white sage, sweetgrass and cedar, which can be obtained from most alternative or New Age stores. When lit, they smoulder slowly and produce clouds of fragrant smoke. This smoke can be used for smudging, or just to scent a room with natural incense. When smudging, the smoke is wafted over the body using a smudge fan, or just a single feather.

Smudging a Place

You can smudge places and objects as well as people. The smoke from smudging will help to cleanse or purify a small area of a room or an entire building, and can also be used on an object, perhaps before using it in a ceremony. When you first move into a new home, smudging can help clear any residual influences of the previous occupants, especially if you can perform it when the place is empty. Whenever or wherever you feel it is appropriate, smudging can be performed.

    The principle is the same as that for smudging a person: cover the whole area and try to feel if there are any particular areas that need a little extra attention. You can finish off by drawing a circle in the air with the fan to close the ritual and seal the cleansing.

Smudging can be used to cleanse an area or place.

Smudging a Person

When used to clean a person's aura, the smoke from the smouldering herbs acts like the soap when washing, picking up the negative grime that accumulates. Following the same analogy, the wind from the fan acts like the water, in that it carries away the grime as it blows through the aura and leaves the smudgee feeling refreshed and uplifted.

    Light the smudge stick and use a smudge fan or feather to fan it until glowing strongly. While smudging, focus on the cleansing action of the herbs and hold the intent of cleansing the recipient in your mind as you perform the act. Imagine the smoke carrying away the grubbiness as it blows through the aura.

1 Your partner should stand with arms outspread, focusing on the cleansing. Fan the smoke over the body, starting at the head and finishing with the feet.

2 When you feel the ritual is complete, finish it by stroking down the aura with the fan, ending each stroke with a flick to preen the aura and signal the end.

shamanic ritual

We are all creatures of habit, with certain ways of performing routine tasks, but what differentiates habit from ritual is intent. Performing an act with conscious intent increases its efficiency, because the intent carries to other levels of your being. If you take a shower with the intent of cleansing your spirit as well as your body, the overall cleansing effect will be greater. Rituals help strengthen our connection with the universe.

Morning Ritual

Greeting the morning is a great way to start a new day. Work out your own simple ritual involving a few stretches followed by a moment of quiet or meditation to collect yourself for the day. If you can be outside, your morning ritual will have greater significance. The yoga moves called "Salute to the Sun" require little time or space and the movements invigorate the body while the ritual strengthens the spiritual bond you have with creation.

Eating as Ritual

Food preparation and eating are powerfully symbolic activities, and a good time to incorporate ritual. Prepare food with love and appreciation of what is supplied by the bountiful Mother.

Eat natural foods in preference to processed ones, and organically produced food in preference to intensively farmed products. This is not only beneficial to your health but also to your spirit. Fresh, organic foods have more goodness and flavour, and a closer connection with the earth, therefore more of those attributes are entering your body. As you prepare food, endow it with love and appreciation every step of the way, and do the same when you eat it. While eating, the food nourishes the body and the ritual nourishes the spirit.

Greeting the day outside has particular significance.

The Breath of Life

Deep-breathing exercises help to awaken a sleep-fuddled mind and vitalize the body. Scoop up armfuls of energy as you breathe in. As you repeat this sequence, begin to visualize a flow of energy, so that you are both gathering it in and giving it out, returning it to its source. Visualize gathering energy in your arms as they rise up above your head and, as you exhale, picture the energy filtering through your aura as you let your arms sink slowly down with your hands.

The fundamental characteristic of energy is movement, and if it is blocked it becomes stagnant in much the same way that still water does. By giving out you are allowing room for more to come in: the more you give, the more you will receive.

1 Stand relaxed with knees slightly flexed and arms at your sides, hands cupped loosely in front of you. Slowly take three deep breaths to centre yourself.

2 On the fourth breath, circle your arms up, keeping them rounded. Now exhale, and let your arms sink slowly down with your hands in front of you as before.

shamanic offerings

When you make an offering you are exchanging energy, as well as giving thanks. Leave an offering on your altar with gratitude for the day and your life. Tobacco is often used, as it is regarded as sacred by native Americans and is used in their ceremonies. Salt, which is regarded as sacred by Celts, is also used for offerings. It doesn't matter what you leave, as long as it is significant to you, and your intent is clear.

Making an Offering Inside

Your indoor altar may be permanently set up in a corner of your home that you have set aside for this purpose, or it may be a very simple collection of stones, candles and incense that you assemble when you feel it is needed.

Use your altar for offerings at particular times of the day, or leave an offering whenever you feel it is right to do so. A good ritual before you go to bed each night is to give thanks for the day that has passed, and to ask for dreams in the coming night to be clear and that you may remember them. Make an offering on your altar last thing at night, using incense and candles, and voice your request aloud to reinforce the intent with which you perform the ritual.

An offering of tobacco on an indoor altar.

Making an Offering Outside

Natural items can be used for offerings, such as a pretty shell or pebble, a single flower or a few nuts or berries that you have gathered on a country walk.

You can leave an offering on an outdoor altar, such as a log or a flat stone, which may be a temporary altar or a place that you visit regularly. As you make your offering, keep in mind your sense of the connection in spirit between yourself and everything else in creation.

Present your offering to Mother Earth, to the sky and to the four directions before leaving it in your chosen place. Say these words as you place it on your altar: "I offer this in gratitude for the gifts given, in honour of creation and my part in it." Speaking aloud helps to focus your attention and energy.

1 To make an offering, gently hold whatever you wish to give in your hand and present it up to the sky.

2 Lower your hand and present your offering to the earth to show appreciation to the Mother.

A stone left as an impromptu offering on a tree.

3 Hold it out to each of the four directions, north, south, east and west.

4 As you leave the offering in your chosen place, voice your thanks and intention.

shamanic symbols

People have used symbols for millennia, as charms for luck, protection and inspiration. Every symbol has its own energetic vibration, which influences the spirit. In ancient rock art, there are certain symbols that appear repeatedly in many places and from many periods, indicating their universal importance for the human spirit. Among these powerful signs, or sigils, are the spiral and the circle in their various forms.

The Role of Symbols

Rock art has been found all over the world, some as much as 35,000 years old. Before writing was developed, information was passed on orally, but our ancestors used symbolic representations to reinforce aspects of their lives, such as successful hunting or good harvests, using positive visualizations. Certain symbols, such as masks or totems, were boundary markers. Other scenes show human figures with animal characteristics, representative of shapeshifting in shamanic journeys, where a shaman will adopt an animal form for learning, healing or communication.

Symbolism remains powerful today, from graffiti to national flags, from religious icons to currency signs and club insignia: each one is a symbol that conveys a wealth of meaning.

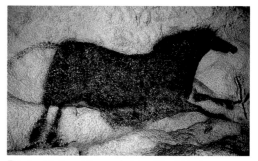

The cave paintings at Lascaux include wild, galloping horses.

The Medicine Wheel

Also known as the sacred hoop, the medicine wheel is used to help meditation. It is a circle bisected by two lines, which symbolize the blue road of spirit (east to west) and the red road of life (south to north). The resulting four sections of the circle represent the seasons. Each cardinal point is associated with particular attributes. The east is the place of inspiration and the inception of a new idea. The south is related to consolidation of the cycle. West is the place where the fruits of an endeavour can be harvested. North is the place to recuperate and reflect.

The circle can help you find the best course of action to take: to decide whether you should be starting something new, or to concentrate on nurturing what you have at present, accepting gains from a situation or drawing your strength in.

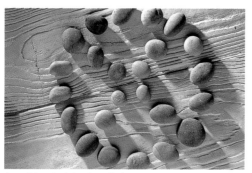

A medicine wheel simply marked out in stones.

Spirals and Circles

The spiral is an evocative image, symbolic of a life path that is moving simultaneously out and around. It relates both to the cyclic nature of existence, and to spiritual and emotional growth through life, apparently repeating experiences, but always moving to new levels. The spiral is also representative of a pathway, usually downwards and inwards, that a shaman may take to reach another realm.

The circle is the line without end. It represents birth, death and rebirth, all intimately linked. The circle symbolizes the cycles which are present in all of creation, the relentless progress of life in all its forms. Circles that incorporate another solid circle inside, speak of the totality of creation, showing that all things are connected and that creation encompasses the individual.

Triple spirals relate to three life stages: maiden, mother and crone.

shamanic tools

The shaman can use a number of natural tools, to assist in connecting with the spirit that weaves through creation. A feather can assist a shaman to fly on a journey; a staff or wand cut from a certain tree can allow insights into the properties of that tree; a stone or crystal can give access to the strength and wisdom of the earth. Other tools are hand-made for specific purposes, and the most universal are the drum and the rattle.

Natural items can be potent shamanic tools.

The Shaman's Drum

The drum carries deep primal undertones that reach into the atavistic recesses of the soul. The heartbeat is the first sound the unborn child hears and the drumbeat evokes the link between mother and child. But it reaches deeper and, representative of the heartbeat of Mother Earth, is full of vibrancy and energy.

The most desirable drum is one you have made yourself by hand, using natural materials, which holds the energy of both the materials and its maker. Make an offering to the drum's spirit before using it for a ceremony, ritual or journey. When journeying, a drum helps to focus the traveller in entering the spirit body. Research indicates that the optimum drumbeat is around 200 beats per minute (bpm), so practise your drumming until this is your automatic rhythm.

Smudge fans can be elaborate or simple.

The Shaman's Rattle

A rattle is a useful tool to signal intent to any spirit you may wish to call upon. Because of this, using a rattle is a good way to open a ceremony or ritual, in addition to voicing your desire aloud. Shamans use it to great effect to coax a damp sweatlodge fire into roaring life by calling on the spirit of the fire. Of course it is also a good complement to any singing and chanting that may occur to you. The rattle can be used for healing purposes, to call in allies to aid with a problem or cure. A very simple rattle can be made by putting dried peas in a jar or tin but, as with the drum, you can buy one, or you may be able to find a workshop where you can learn to make one from hide mounted on a wooden handle and filled with dried beans or pebbles.

In journeying, the drumbeat opens gateways to other worlds.

Smudge Fan

A smudge fan is a very simple tool to make and is very pleasing to use. It can be as elaborate or as simple as you wish, consisting of feathers mounted on a handle or just bundled together and decorated with small beads and bells. Feathers make very good smudge fans and have the advantage of holding within them some of the energy of the birds that gave them. For example, eagles and associated birds of prey symbolize the ability to fly high and see far; owls, with their renowned night vision, represent the ability to see inside or beyond the veil of reality; ravens and crows have a long history of occult links; turkeys symbolize abundance. You can always find feathers while out walking in the country, so pick them up and see if they convey any sense of their properties to you.

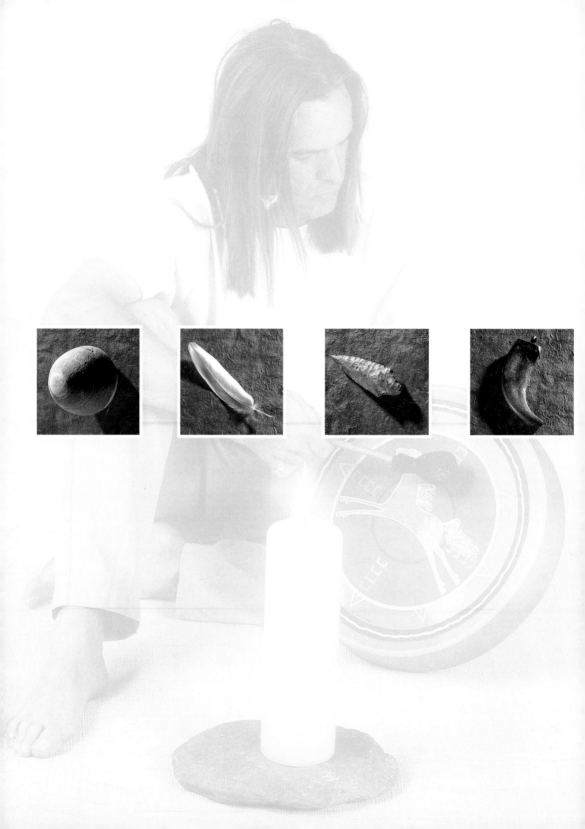

dreamworlds and journeys

dreamworlds and journeys

To enter a dreamworld is to enter a place where anything can happen. It is a magical world of limitless possibilities, where the dreamer will find that they can fly, shapeshift, walk through solid objects or swim in the sun. And, especially while the dream is going on, it is every bit as real as this common reality that we all share from day to day.

A dream is a way for the spirit self to communicate with the physical body, relaying information in allegorical frames that relate to the dreamer's life and experiences. Because the inner dreamworld reflects the outer world of the dreamer, it follows that a change in the outer world will result in a change in the inner dreamworld.

To go a step further, because all worlds are dreams, a change in the inner dreamworld will effect a change in this outer world. This idea that we all dream our own world into existence is not a new one, and if we are the creators of that reality we must then, by extension, have the ability to change it by changing the dream. Dreaming is an important human activity and changing a dream is a self-empowering way of altering circumstances, behaviour and responses. A shaman recognizes the validity of those other worlds and also accepts that this world, which we inhabit, is the dreamscape of some other reality. This is how strong, experienced shamans can perform magical or superhuman feats; they can enter other worlds at will and project them to such an extent that they can be experienced by an observer.

We all have the ability to journey to different worlds: indeed, this is what we are doing each night when we dream. These otherworlds are places of limitless possibilities, where information is relayed in a format the journeyer can relate to. But in shamanic journeying, unlike dreams, the journey to a different world is undertaken with conscious intent and with a specific goal in mind, such as healing or to gain new insight. The journey can begin in your own sacred space. When journeying to another realm it is important to be open to whatever may happen and to anything you might meet. Trust your intuition, because what first comes to you is the right thing, whatever it may be. Just go with the flow and don't try to force anything.

working with dreams
To work with a dream with a view to changing or interpreting it, you need to return to it by recalling it while relaxed and conscious. Being relaxed allows your intuition to flow more freely and enables you to use your creativity to a greater degree. It is this interplay of intuitive creativity that allows you to gain insights from dreams and to effect a beneficial change in them, enabling you to move forward.

Dream Interpretation

The information that dreams are trying to convey can be divined by the simple expedient of questioning whoever or whatever is in the dream. If you can practise lucid dreaming, the questions can be posed there and then. If not, ask them in recollection.

To determine whether or not you can dream lucidly, try to perform a voluntary act in the dream. Attempt something simple, such as looking down at your hands or feet. Just work with it and see what can be done. If you wake with the memory of a dream, run through it to help fix it or, even better, write it down immediately. If possible, go back to it there and then, although it can be done at a later date.

When you are back in your dream, politely question the characters and even the places involved. Go with the first answer that comes to mind but don't accept "No". A character may run or try to frighten you but don't be intimidated. Follow them if necessary – they will lead you to an answer.

More often than not, the main characters in a dream are manifestations of aspects of the dreamer. For example, disturbing dreams – perhaps involving death or violence of some kind – are not necessarily portents that some harm is about to befall the

Dreaming is an important activity.

characters involved. Rather, the injured parties represent aspects of the dreamer that are being harmed, perhaps by not being allowed their full expression.

Record your dreams in a journal for future reference and because they can offer valuable insights. Keep a pad by your bed so that you can write dreams down when they are fresh, because they tend to slip away from the wakening mind very easily.

Returning to a Dream

If you want to return to a dream that seemed particularly significant or curious to you, you can use these simple steps to focus your mind on the dream and explore it. In doing this you may well find that you can then release it.

1 Perform a small ritual beforehand: light candles as a symbol of the inner illumination that will help to guide you back into your dream.

2 Make an offering and voice your intent. Why are you returning to the dream? For understanding? To change it? Or to extend it?

3 Sit or lie comfortably and relax yourself with deep diaphragmatic breathing. Start the dream again and focus on what occurs.

changing dreams

The self-empowering ability to change your dreams has effects in this world, according to the shamanic premise that all worlds are in fact dreamscapes. Invariably, the dreams that we want to change are those that cause a response of fear, pain or anger in us, and by taking control over them in the dreamworld they manifest in, we are affirming our strength here, in the physical, conscious world.

Deciding what to Change

There are a number of ways in which you can change dreams. If the dreams are complete they can be altered by changing what occurs in them or by changing how you, the dreamer, react to what goes on. If the dream is incomplete it can be continued with creative intuition.

When changing a dream don't try to force things to happen, just let your intuition flow and allow your creativity to come to the fore. Remember, anything can happen in a dream, so don't restrict yourself to the physical constraints of this world.

Changing what Occurs

Say you have a dream in which you feel powerless, perhaps chasing someone or something which eludes you. A way of changing that type of dream is actually to catch whatever it is that you are pursuing. They may continue to escape when you re-enter the dream, but be persistent and persevere until you reach your goal. This is a self-empowerment technique which returns the control to you. When you can confront whatever eludes you, it may lead to an altogether unexpected insight.

Belinda's Dream *by Henry Fuseli.*

Changing your Response

In a similar way to changing the dream, changing your response is a method of taking control. Fear dreams are often recurrent, and many feature being chased or stalked by some unseen or barely glimpsed presence. This can cause a great deal of anxiety and the dreamer may wake up short of breath and with a pounding heart. A way of taking control in this situation would be to transmute the reaction: instead of being tense and afraid in the dream, be lighthearted and happy. This will help dispel anxiety.

Extending a Dream

Most of us have experienced dreams that end prematurely when we wake, usually with a fearful start. A good way of changing this type of dream is to allow it to continue and see where it goes. Simply recall the dream and, at the point where you woke up, carry it on using your creative intuition.

A typical situation in this type of dream is that the dreamer is falling, which can signify a leap into the unknown. The dream usually ends abruptly just before impact with the ground (thank goodness), but who knows what might happen if the dream was allowed to continue? Perhaps the ground might open up to allow safe passage, or maybe it would turn out to be soft and resilient. A good way to find out is to return to the dream, allow your creative intuition free rein and take that leap.

A Dream of the East *by Jean-Jules Antoine Lecomte.*

journeying

Unique to shamanism, the practice of journeying is a very powerful way to gain insights into problems, to look for healing, to seek allies or just to relax. When you journey, you enter a different world. It is essentially one that you create and guide yourself through, although your conscious self relinquishes control to your spirit. We have already explored the concept of sacred space and this is a good place to start a journey.

Contemplating a Journey

When journeying to another realm, it is important to be open to whatever may happen and to anything you might meet. Trust your intuition, because what first comes to you is the right thing, whatever it may be. Just go with the flow and don't try to force anything. Remember that you have control over what you can accomplish in this otherworld that you have travelled to and don't be inhibited by fear. Be creative in circumventing any problems and challenges that may arise.

The Role of the Drum

A drum is useful in journeying and it is good to have someone drum for you, as a regular rhythm of around 200 beats per minute aids the focus needed for the opening of a gateway. It is good to build up the rhythm gradually to allow the traveller to become acclimatized to the adventure.

At first it is best to journey for a set time of around five minutes. At the end of this period the drummer can initiate the return by changing the rhythm to give a call-back signal — for example, four one-second beats followed by some very rapid drumming. With experience, the drummer will be able to use their intuition to tell when the traveller's journey is complete. If you are drumming for someone else, your power animal might

Make your own drumming tape if you have no one to drum for you.

be able to tell you when to start the call-back. Making a drumming tape to accompany your journeys can also be very useful, as you can record several drumming sessions of various lengths and incorporate your own call-back signal.

Preparing for a Journey

As with physical travel in this world, if you prepare properly for a spiritual journey, things will go much more smoothly and it will be a much more relaxing and fruitful experience. A simple ritual helps to prepare you by centring you and focusing your attention on the journey you are about to undertake.

Gather your tools together and create a comfortable place where you feel relaxed and safe from disturbance. Light a candle for inner illumination and contemplate it quietly for a while.

As you make your offering, call upon the spirit of the drum to assist you on your journey and express your gratitude for the help you are receiving.

1 Smudge yourself, the tools and your surroundings. Make an offering to the spirit of the drum and voice your intent, for example to meet a power animal or find a power object on your journey.

2 Lie comfortably and breathe deeply to relax. Start the tape, and compose yourself as the drumming begins, maintaining deep, regular breaths as your journey commences.

power animals

Your can make a journey to meet your own personal spirit ally, which takes the form of an animal. It is an ally that can accompany you on future journeys and give you guidance and wisdom. Animals have always had great significance to native peoples all over the world and throughout history. In any culture, certain animals are thought to embody traits and strengths that are relevant to the history and geography of the culture.

The eagle flies high, symbolizing the striving for higher goals.

The Symbolism of Power Animals

Whole books have been written on the symbolism of animals. This list represents a few of the more common ones. Nowadays, we are familiar with animals from all over the world, and you may meet a power animal that has no general cultural significance, but the important thing is what that spirit represents to you. What strengths does it convey? What does it teach you?

Eagle: can fly high and free without fear and has the gift of far-sightedness. It symbolizes restless male energy, striving for higher goals. Similar totems include the buzzard and condor.
Bear: retreats in winter to hibernate and renew its earth connection. It represents receptive female energy, able to go within to seek answers. A similar totem is the badger.
Wolf: fiercely loyal and true, still maintains its freedom and independence. A similar totem is the hound or dog.
Coyote: related to the wolf, exhibits the trust, innocence and playfulness of the child in all of us.
Bison: evokes the strength and wisdom of the elders, providers for and protectors of the people. Similar totems include the bull, reindeer and orca.
Horse: covers distance with endurance, symbolizing swiftness, freedom and faithfulness. A similar totem is the elk.
Dolphin: represents understanding and awareness, with a gentle, loving energy. Similar totems are the manatee and deer.
Owl: hunts by night. Symbolically it represents the ability to see that which is indistinct and understand hidden truths.

Journey to Meet a Power Animal

Meeting a power animal is a useful journey to start with because the animal can accompany you on future adventures. It is not a deep journey but it does expand your awareness, taking you to the edge of your sacred space, where it borders the realms of other spirits. Once you have prepared for your journey, enter your spirit body, go to your sacred space and orient yourself.

Begin walking. As you do so, a path will become apparent. Follow the path to the boundary of your sacred space. Take your time to acclimatize yourself and observe your surroundings. Wait, because the ally will come to you.

The animal could be anything and it may not be what you were expecting, but when it arrives, greet it warmly, touch it and give it love. Be aware of what it feels like and feel the love it has for you. Remember, the greater the detail, the more real it will seem. If it feels appropriate, transform yourself into the same animal and run, fly or swim. Above all, have some fun.

When you hear the call-back signal, thank the animal for coming and tell it you look forward to future meetings. Retrace your steps and return to the familiar area of your sacred space before leaving it and coming back to awareness of this world.

When you have returned, go over the journey in your mind or write it down to help fix the details. This will aid you in future travels and make it easier to access the next time you visit.

Follow the path to the boundaries of your sacred space.

journeys to otherworlds

Deeper journeys to otherworlds require going beyond your sacred space. The otherworlds that shamans journey to are many and varied and can encompass any number of features, because each is a construct of the shaman who enters it. Essentially, otherworlds are confined to two realms, and when you journey from your sacred space you can travel downwards to the underworld or upwards to the upperworld.

The Underworld

Most shamanic journeys involve going to the underworld, which is not comparable with the hell of Christianity and other faiths, but represents the inner recesses of the traveller. It is a place of challenges and adventure. A shaman enters the underworld to seek solutions and understanding. The challenges you might encounter are all manifestations of your own fears and problems. By confronting them and finding solutions in the underworld you are facing them within yourself and allowing your spirit to communicate the solutions to your conscious self. Because you are journeying within yourself, you are seeking an entrance that will lead downwards and in. Remember, to gain entry, you can transform yourself to any size and shape required.

At first it is an advantage to have some structure to a journey. A good goal is to meet another shaman, who will give you something. It could be knowledge, such as insight into a problem, or it could be an object. Accept it gratefully and give something in return. If the gift is an object take it back to your sacred space and put it away in a safe place.

The Upperworld

Associated with the higher self or the soul, the upperworld is the place to go to for inspiration and communion with other spirits. Whereas a journey to the underworld is about confronting fears that lie within yourself, the upperworld is more concerned with seeking assistance from others, by meeting other spirits on an equal basis, sharing any knowledge you have gained with them and gaining new insights from them.

This realm is very light and tranquil, with a feeling of limitless space that stretches away forever. Because it is related to the higher self, it is reached by going upwards. As with a journey to the underworld, it is good to have some structure to follow to help maintain your focus so that you do not lose your way. Because going upwards relates to the soul, a good focus to have is to connect with your higher self. This is the part of your being that is calm and all-knowing. It is dissociated from the emotions that have such a strong influence on the physical body, and can therefore give you counsel with a dispassionate objectivity that will cut to the heart of a problem.

Entrances to the Underworld

- A cave or crevice in the side of a rockface;
- A recess or a knothole in a tree;
- A wormhole;
- An animal's burrow in a bank;
- A well;
- A doorway or gate;
- A waterfall or stream.

Entrances to the Upperworld

- A gap in the sky which can be reached by flying or leaping;
- A cave mouth high up a cliff that you need to scale;
- A tall tree to climb;
- A mountain that pierces a cloud;
- A flight of stairs;
- A ladder.

After passing through the opening, take note of your surroundings.

The upperworld is a peaceful, tranquil place.

journeying for others

Sometimes a shaman may be required to journey on behalf of someone else, for healing or to seek the answer to a question. The principle is always the same: go with a specific aim in mind and be open to what befalls you on the way to your goal. The meaning of the tests and solutions might not be immediately apparent, but ideas will manifest themselves to the conscious mind and answers will come.

On your journey to find another soul, your path may not be clear, but keep following and it will eventually lead you to your goal.

Soul Retrieval Journey

Journeying on behalf of another person is a mutually beneficial undertaking and can form a close bond between the two people involved. Sometimes a person may be too deeply involved in an issue, or too traumatized, to journey with clarity for themselves. Someone else, removed from the immediacy of the situation, is likely to be more successful in the venture, being able to see with a more objective eye.

A journey to find part of a person's soul is a beautiful journey to undertake for someone else. As the name suggests, the purpose is to return a part of the soul or spirit to its rightful place. We are often careless with our soul: as we go through life we may leave a part of it with someone else or even lose a part during difficult times of our lives. These lost pieces of our soul are of no use to anyone else, but the result is that we are left less than complete – weakened in such a way that it can take a long time to recover. By restoring an errant piece of soul to where it belongs, the healing process is facilitated and the recipient becomes more resilient.

Because you are journeying for someone else, it is beneficial to develop an empathy with that person, so an extra step is incorporated into your preparation. Sit quietly for about ten minutes holding hands with the other person and feeling each other's energy, then perform the preparation ritual. Relax by

breathing deeply, enter your spirit body and go to your sacred space. Call for, and greet, your power animal, who will be your ally on the journey. You are seeking another's soul so the journey will take you upwards into the upperworld. Begin walking along the path and look for the entrance. Once in the upperworld, locate the main part of the soul and note the missing area. Is it raw like a cut or has it healed like a scar?

Begin your search for the missing piece of the soul. It could have become attached to someone else's soul, or it could be wandering alone. You may find that it seems lost and afraid or it may be comfortable and happy where it is.

Once you have found it, talk to it. Find out what part of the soul it is and why it left or was given away. Tell it that it has a rightful place where it is needed. Be persuasive and do not leave without it. When it agrees to accompany you, guide it back to where it belongs and see it settled back in and comfortable before you leave.

Retrace your steps to your sacred space, say goodbye to your ally and come back to awareness of this world. Relate the events you have experienced in detail to the person you made the journey for and, if they agree, record your experiences in your journal to help you recall them later.

Spend some time before you start your preparation for your journey "tuning-in" to the person you are journeying for.

further journeying

When seeking an answer to a problem either travel into yourself to find a shaman who can share wisdom with you or travel up to meet your higher self for a dispassionate opinion, presenting what is best for you with clarity and insight. You are actively seeking an answer on these journeys so remember to be respectful and loving to whoever you meet and to trust your intuition.

Journey to Meet a Shaman

As with all journeys, begin by performing the preparation ritual to focus your intent. State your reasons for going and request the help you might need.

Relax with breathing, enter your spirit body and go to your sacred space. Call for, and greet, your power animal. Begin walking and, as you do, look for that opening that leads down and in, and enter the underworld. Once you have entered, be aware of your surroundings as you follow the path to the shaman.

If you are confronted by obstacles or opponents, find a way around them or through them and do not allow them to bar your passage. Be as creative as possible in getting past anything that may stand in your way. Remember, you have control over yourself and that your power animal can help you. When you meet the shaman, be respectful and loving. Whatever they give you is precious, whether it is an object or an answer to a question, and should be received by you with gratitude.

When it is time to return, retrace your steps, find the path and get back to your sacred space. Put any gifts you may have received somewhere safe and say goodbye to your ally. Leave your sacred space and come back to awareness of this world.

Record the events in a journal, because the information given may not be immediately apparent and you may wish to read through it again at a later date.

A cave or crevice is a classic entrance to the underworld. Follow it down to gain access to your inner recesses.

Your higher self is calm and all-knowing. It can be found in the tranquil reaches of the upper world.

Journey to Meet your Higher Self

Before you begin the journey to meet your higher self, follow the preparation ritual and state your intent. Relax by breathing deeply, enter your spirit body and go to your sacred space. Call for, and greet, your ally.

Begin walking, looking for the entrance to the upperworld, and enter. Once there, pause and take a moment to observe your surroundings. Your soul might be right there or you may have to go in search of it.

When you meet your higher self, greet it with love. It is wise beyond words and only wants what is best for the whole of you. Pose any questions you may have and receive the answers gratefully. They might not be what your physical body wants to hear but they will be honest.

When it is time to return to this world, thank your higher self for the meeting and retrace your steps back to your sacred space. Say goodbye to your power animal and come back to awareness of this world.

Record the journey and any insights you may have been given to help clarify them and for future reference.

an account of a journey

This extract from a dream journal describes an eventful and exciting journey, which the shaman consciously and deliberately undertakes to explore a problem that has been worrying him. The dreamworld's allegorical framework helps him to understand his problem and to change this world when he returns. As you will see, he gains valuable insight from his travels.

The Dream Journal – an extract

...We followed a path with trees on either side. They twined together overhead, growing thicker, until the tree-tunnel became a shaft sloping into the Earth, big enough to walk down. It was roughly oval and felt warm and dry. We emerged from a hole in a bank and looked around.

The bank extended to the left and right and a forest of pine trees crowded thickly up against it. My ally, the wolf, walked forwards and I saw that he had found a path. I followed him and we snaked among the trees until we came to a small clearing. Suddenly, a giant face appeared, childlike but with curly blond hair and a beard, tilted to one side with curiosity. It looked through the trees as if through the bars of a cage and reached out a groping hand. I thought about running but stopped myself and waited to see what would happen. The hand scooped us up and popped us into the creature's open mouth.

The path through the trees leads the shaman to another world.

We scooted down a long, dark tunnel and were ejected on to a wide, snowy plain, flanked on either side by mountains. It felt great to be running together through the snow. We reached the edge of a sheer cliff, so high that there were clouds below us. We stood looking out over an ocean and could see an island in the distance, small and green. How could we reach it?

A huge eagle swooped down and seized us. Its talons were sharp and powerful but they held us gently. Then the eagle was gone and we were gliding down on our own, heading for the island.

We landed in a marketplace, crowded with brightly clad people who paid us no attention. I thought one of them must be able to answer my question and I began asking at random. Everyone ignored me and I began to feel frustrated and angry, until my ally grasped my arm in his teeth and pulled me towards a narrow alley. He let go and looked at me before turning and walking into the dim interior, beckoning me to follow him with a growl.

The brick walls of the alley became the rock walls of a canyon which led to a cave. An old man sat watching us from the entrance. He stood up as we reached him and I asked the question again. He made no reply but touched his index finger to his forehead and then to my forehead. He held up a small mirror to my face and then I saw a blue mark where his finger had touched me.

I thanked him and we moved on into the cave. When we came out we were back in my sacred space. The wolf was no longer at my side and I looked over my shoulder to see him standing between two trees. I went back to say goodbye and he bared his teeth at me (a smile or a warning?) before turning and melting into the undergrowth.

The wolf is a powerful spirit ally. Fiercely loyal, it still retains its independence.

What Does it Mean?

The shaman's journey, shows (apart, very simply, from what a good time you can have on a journey) that the question that was troubling his mind had assumed gigantic proportions and was literally swallowing him up. Additionally, the shaman had been bothering too many other people for an answer, when all he had to do was look inside himself. And the bared teeth at the end? That was just the wolf laughing.

Surrounded by sea - the unconscious - the island can provide clarity and answers.

receiving a power object

While you are making a journey, you may receive a power object, something that is for healing, inspiration or empowerment. This may be the gift of a shaman whom you meet, or your path may lead you to it. The object itself, once found, should be brought back to your sacred space and left there, but the spirit or energy of it is brought back to this common reality and kept with you.

Journey to Find a Power Object

The power object may take any form. It may be a natural object, or something that has been made from natural materials, carrying the energy of the maker within it. Its significance may become apparent only later, after you have returned from your journey.

Of course, when you obtain the power object, you should remember to leave something in exchange, because that strengthens the link. An offering in this case works the other way around: you leave the physical offering in this world, and you take the spirit of it with you into your sacred space when you make a journey. Making this offering can be incorporated into your preparation ritual as an extra step.

To find a power object, perform the now familiar ritual of preparation, then make your offering to signify the grateful receipt of the object you seek, taking the spirit of the offering with you. Sit or lie down comfortably, relax by breathing deeply, enter your spirit body and go to your sacred space. Call for, and greet, your ally. Power objects are found in the underworld, so look for the opening, enter and look around you.

In the underworld, look for a path or let your ally guide you to the object you seek. Do not allow obstacles or opponents to hinder you on your quest. Be adaptable in circumventing problems and keep an open mind. When you find the object, receive it gratefully and leave the spirit offering. Retrace your path back to your sacred space and leave the power object in a safe place. Thank your ally and say goodbye, then return to this world.

When you have received a power object on a journey, be aware of things that may come to you in this world, objects which may be a physical representation of the power object that you left in your sacred space. These things may not look like the article that was given to you, but they will have a similar feel, or energy, about them. They are often gifts from other people, but they could be things you see when you are out walking, or even while you are shopping. The key is to be aware.

A power object can be natural or man-made or a combination of the two. It will have an energy that is derived from the earth, or the animal from which it comes, or from its maker, and you may recognize this energy in objects you encounter in the physical world when you return from your journey. Some examples of power objects are, anticlockwise from top left: smooth, river-washed stone, eagle feather (or other bird's feather), flint arrowhead, deer antler, bear claw pendant.

receiving a symbol

Symbols are potent images, and it probably won't surprise you to learn that, as a shaman, you can discover or create your own symbols for personal empowerment. Returning to the idea that dreamworlds and reality are essentially the same, symbols that appear in dreams and journeys have their own reality and strength. Any symbol that you receive on a journey or in a dream can be represented physically in this world.

Journey to Find a Symbol

In essence, a power animal is a symbol, as is a power object, and just as you journeyed to find an ally or an object, a similar journey can be undertaken to discover a particular symbol to aid you in healing or self-empowerment. Such a symbol could take any form: a word, a picture, a song, a design or even a person. The important thing is that it is significant to you and that it conveys a strength that you can call upon.

After your journey, you can give physical form to the symbol you received. For example, a design or an image can be drawn; a word or phrase can be written down. These images can be displayed around your home so that you can focus your attention on them to gain the benefits they offer. A song can be sung whenever necessary for the same purpose, and a person can be represented by a drawing or even a photograph.

Whatever forms your symbols take, you need to focus your attention on them to get the maximum benefits. It is not enough just to have them lying around. If the symbol is an image, spend time each day concentrating on it; if it is a word, phrase or song, say it aloud or read it, and if it's solid, handle it and note its detail.

Visualizing a Symbol

You don't need to go on a journey to create a symbol but you do need to be in a relaxed state to let your creative intuition flow freely and to contact your higher self. Symbols are a form of positive visualization, so you need to focus on an area of your life where you would like to see some improvement, such as a new job or a different lifestyle.

Once you have the concept in mind, perform a simple ritual to help focus your attention. When you start receiving images or words, write them down or draw them as they come. Don't worry about fine details at this stage, because the main thing you are after is the form, and you can embellish it later. When you have finished, thank your higher self for helping you and see what you have come up with.

There is no limit to the number of symbols that you can acquire or create, although if you have too many you may become a bit confused about what you are trying to achieve. As with a power object, you need to be aware of things that come to you later that may have a similar feel to them, things that may represent your symbol in this world.

Receiving a Symbol

In order to find a symbol to help you in your quest, you must simply follow the steps below. Create a soothing atmosphere and quietly focus your mind on what it is that you wish to achieve and hold this vision in your mind's eye.

1 To begin your preparation ritual, light a candle to represent inner illumination. Relax and make yourself comfortable as you sit and contemplate the candle flame for a while.

2 Smudge yourself with purifying herbs to cleanse and calm you. Also smudge the tools you will be using to give form to your symbol, and the place where you will be sitting.

3 Holding a pad and pencil, close your eyes. Breathe deeply and concentrate on your objective. Ask your higher self to give you a symbol that will help you to achieve your aim.

dream therapy

dream therapy
dream therapy

By their very nature, dreams are ephemeral and transitory, and therefore difficult to remember. If you do remember them it is often in the form of a confused series of images and feelings, but occasionally a dream is so startlingly vivid that it stays with you for hours, sometimes days, afterwards. To dismiss the significance of dreams and the role they play would be to ignore a regular experience that is not only fascinating but can also be insightful and inspiring. There are ways to help you remember your dreams and lead you to a greater understanding of them. This in turn could lead to a greater understanding of the events that affect and influence your waking life.

Dream analysis is not straightforward. The dream language of symbols and images needs to be interpreted. Sometimes the meaning may be obvious, such as a dream about a supervisor at work turning into a monster, but at other times you need to dig deeper, and you may even discover that themes or patterns begin to recur. Sadly, dreams are more often negative than positive (which is why nightmares tend to be more memorable than pleasant dreams), but this is a good reason to try to understand them as they can help you confront and assess unresolved problems.

Dreams are as individual as people. Exploring yours may reveal different aspects of yourself, offer an interesting perspective on life, or fire your imagination and creative potential. It is an unexplored territory waiting to be discovered.

the history of dreams

Dreams have always held a great fascination for us. At different times, and in different cultures, they have been seen as warnings, prophecies or messages from the gods, and they have been bestowed with the power to solve problems, heal sickness and provide spiritual revelation. Methods of dream interpretation change, but our desire to look for the significance in them has remained constant.

The Egyptians

The Ancient Egyptian civilization, which dates back as far as 4000 BC, was probably the first to develop a system of dream interpretation. Dream books listed possible dream scenarios and gave an interpretation. For example a dream about drinking warm beer forewarned that the dreamer would soon suffer harm. Nightmares were guarded against with spells and protective headrests.

A practice, known as "dream incubation", was widespread. Egyptians would sleep in healing sanctuaries in the hope that the gods would send them a message through their dreams. Professional dream interpreters would be at hand.

One of the most well-known dreams from that time was of Thutmose IV, a young prince. He fell asleep under a statue of a sphinx who told him in his dream to sweep the sand from around him and the throne of Egypt would be his.

The Ancient Greeks

The Greeks were very interested in dreams and created a complex dream lore. They made a distinction between "true" and "false" dreams, breaking down the "true" or significant dreams into three categories:

the symbolic dream – in which events appear as metaphors and cannot be understood without interpretation;

the vision dream – seen as a pre-enactment of a future event;

the oracle dream – in which a dream figure reveals what will or will not happen.

The dream stele of Thutmose IV records how he became king.

The Greek poet, Homer, used oracle dreams in his epic poems about the Trojan War, the *Iliad* and the *Odyssey*, both thought to have been written in the 8th century BC. In these epics, dreams often take the form of a visit from a dream figure (a god or a ghost), who appears at the head of the bed and delivers a message to the sleeper, and then usually disappears through a keyhole.

Dreams, in particular oracle dreams, were regarded as messages from the gods and were eagerly sought. Later, the practice of dream incubation was a highly organized activity. The Greeks regarded dreams as a source of healing; sick people in search of a cure would sleep at temples dedicated to Aesculapius, a magical healer-turned-god, who provided healing and medical advice in dreams.

One of the earliest dream-interpretation books was written by the Greek diviner and dream interpreter, Artemidorus, in the 2nd century AD. His five-volume work, the *Oneirocritica* ("The Interpretation of Dreams"), is both a dream dictionary and compilation of Greek dream lore, and includes his own observations on the subject. He was one of the first to realize the importance of taking the dreamer's personality and circumstances into account when interpreting a dream.

A Greek woman asleep, 2nd century BC. The Greeks developed an in-depth dream lore and were forerunners in dream interpretation.

The Aborigines

"Dreamtime" is the term used by the Australian Aborigines to describe the creation of the world by their great mythic ancestors. They believe that their ancestors (giants and animals) sprang from the earth, sea and sky in the Dreamtime to create the landscape, their giant steps forming mountain ranges, rocks and sacred sites.

For centuries Aborigines have followed in their footsteps, as part of a spiritual journey or seasonal tribal migration. Each feature of the landscape, from waterhole to mountain, has meaning and is marked by songs, rituals and legends, which have to be re-enacted at certain times of the year to maintain the order of the land and retain links with the ancestors. Sometimes new information on a "dreaming track" presents itself in a dream, and a new ritual is created. There is little distinction made between waking and dreaming events, and many ceremonies are adopted directly from what has been seen in visions, or in sleep, by special individuals.

There are more than 500 distinct Aboriginal tribal groups in Australia, many of which have diverse explanations of dreams. The Dieri believe that a sleeper can be visited by the spirit of a dead person. The Narrang-ga believe that the spirit can leave the body during sleep and communicate with the spirits of others, or with the spirits of the dead who wander the bush. The Japagalk believe that if someone is ill they can be helped by the visit of a dead friend in a dream.

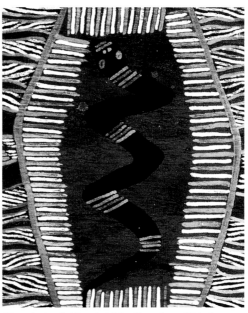

This snake is called "Jaragba". It is a Dreamtime spirit to the Australian Aborigines.

To Australian Aborigines, the landscape was created in Dreamtime, their name for the creation.

Tibetan Buddhists

Buddhism is shaped by the philosophy that the world we experience is unreal or illusory, and the goal of religious or spiritual life is to "wake up" from the illusion. One way in which this "awakening" can take place is through the practice of yoga. In its original southern Asian form, the practice encompasses a variety of exercises, both physical and spiritual, aimed at releasing the individual from the cycle of reincarnation. Although there are many different forms of Buddhism, it was Tibetan Buddhism – which was established in Tibet in 747 AD – that took the practice further by devising a form of yoga to control the dream state. This involves what is commonly known as lucid dreaming – the awareness that you are dreaming while in a dream state. Masters of Tibetan dream yoga are said to be able to pass in and out of sleep without even losing consciousness.

During sleep, the yogi (the person practising yoga) exercises control over the content and direction of their dream, and in so doing becomes aware of the fact that the dream world is transitory and can be manipulated by the power of the conscious mind. This, in turn, will help the yogi realize that the waking world, as well as the dreaming world, is a creation of the mind and therefore also illusory. It is also believed that controlling the dream state helps the yogi to determine where his or her consciousness goes after death – a major goal in schools of Tibetan Buddhism.

Tibetan monks believe that they can control their dreams through the practice of yoga – a form of lucid dreaming.

The Navaho Indians believe that bad dreams always come true although good dreams are only realized once in a while.

The Native Americans

According to the North American Indians, dreams are the most important experience in an individual's life. The meanings of dreams vary from tribe to tribe, but generally the influence of a dream is regarded as good or bad depending on the dream's content and its effect on the dreamer.

The Navaho usually interpret a dream in terms of its influence on the individual. If, for example, a dream has indicated illness then a curing ritual will take place. Dreams are divided into good or bad, and there are rituals to deal with the causes and results of bad dreams, the most common of which is to pray at sunrise. Some dreams are believed to cause sickness and require diagnosis and treatment. Death dreams tend to have standard interpretations. If, for example, a Navaho dreams he is dead, it means that he was visiting the spirits of the dead in the next world. If he shakes hands with the dead, it means that he is going to die. According to the Navaho Indians, good dreams come true only once in a while, but bad dreams always come true.

The Mohave Indians believe that dreams are the basis of everything in life. Their interpretation is that good dreams indicate good luck, and bad dreams mean that bad luck is around the corner. They also believe that shamans, or "medicine men", acquire their powers by dreaming and that they can enter their dreams at will. According to the Kamia of California and Mexico, dreams are better left to the young as old people risk dying during theirs.

The Bible

There are countless examples of dreams in the Bible, which appear as one of the more common forms of communication with God. In Biblical times the Israelites were revered as dream interpreters by the Babylonians and Egyptians. One of the best-known was Joseph, whose story is told in the Book of Genesis. The eleventh and favourite child of Jacob, Joseph was hated by his brothers, who sold him into slavery in Egypt. There Joseph was asked by the Pharaoh to interpret two of his dreams, and he accurately predicted seven years of hunger, but also recommended a plan of action that would save Egypt from famine. The Pharaoh was so impressed that he made Joseph his chief minister. Joseph was consequently honoured by his family, an event he had also foretold in a dream.

The belief that dreams were divinely inspired continued into the early centuries of Christianity, but slowly began to move away from dream interpretation as direct communication and prophecy. In the New Testament, dreams were seen as straightforward messages from God to the disciples. By the Middle Ages, however, it was believed that God's messages could only be received through the Church, thus ruling out the possibility of the ordinary believer receiving divine messages directly from God.

The pharoah dreams of seven thin and seven fat cows – a dream that is interpreted for him by Joseph.

Joseph's father, Jacob, dreamt that a ladder ascended to heaven where the Lord appeared and promised land to his chosen people.

the psychology of dreams

In the past, as we have seen, people believed that dreams were brought to them by an external force and had some meaning beyond the purely personal. So, it wasn't until the advent of psychoanalysis at the end of the 19th century that our perspective changed and we understood that dreams, and their meaning, come from within the unconscious. Two of the most influential pioneers working in the field of dream analysis were Sigmund Freud and Carl Jung.

Sigmund Freud's methods of free association and interpretation of dreams formed the basic techniques of psychoanalysis.

Sigmund Freud (1856–1939)

Freud believed that dreams were manifestations of repressed desires (usually sexual in nature) dating back to early childhood, and that the best way to explore and understand them was through psychoanalysis. The basis of Freud's psychoanalytic theory was the belief that most of our adult behaviour is determined by early childhood experiences, especially sexual, and that if these experiences are painful we bury them in our unconscious mind. When we sleep, this repressed material enters our conscious mind in the form of dreams. However, since these desires are often shocking or threatening, they enter the conscious mind in a disguised, symbolic form. The symbols mask the true meaning of the dream, which can only be reached once they have been interpreted and understood.

The technique Freud used to reach this understanding and interpretation was "free association". He encouraged the patient, or dreamer, to express anything that came to mind, beginning with a symbol, for example a car, that had appeared in his dream. To try it, think of a symbol, then allow your mind to wander through any words that come into your head and see where the train of thought takes you, for example the symbol might lead to: road – travel – holiday – Scotland – walks – healthy – refreshed.

Freud believed that this chain of association leads to the source of the unconscious problem or hidden meaning.

Freud's ground-breaking work on the analysis of dreams opened the door to many seeking access to the meaning of dreams.

Carl Jung (1875–1961)

Jung worked closely with Freud until 1913, when their different approaches to dream analysis caused a rift between them. Like Freud, Jung believed that dreams could reveal the source of unconscious problems but he didn't believe that all dreams came from unconscious conflicts, or that the conflicts (and the symbols that represented them) were sexual. He believed that many symbols could only be interpreted and understood in relation to the dreamer's own experience, and could not be given fixed meanings. He also preferred to look at a series of dreams, rather than an individual dream, to see if a theme developed which could be important for the dreamer's personal growth.

Jung also believed that many dreams contained symbols which, on the surface, appeared meaningless to the dreamer. These came from what he called the "collective unconscious" – a memory bank of thoughts, feelings and images shared by all humans from all cultures, which have meaning for everyone. This inherited memory bank manifests itself in universal symbols, images and stories, called "archetypes", which emerge repeatedly in fairytales, myths, fantasies and religions and reflect our basic human desires and experiences. For Jung, dream analysis was an invaluable tool for self-discovery and personal development rather than a method for unearthing past traumas.

Jung believed that thoughts and associations should always refer directly back to the symbol. To try this for yourself, write down the symbol, for example – car, hold it in your mind, then write down all the associated ideas that come to you, constantly referring back to the original symbol, for example wheels – engine – speed – fast – control – power. Then move on to the next symbol and make a list for that one. You will find that certain themes will recur and certain symbols will become familiar. In time, you will learn to understand your own dream language.

Carl Jung worked closely with Freud until 1913, when he began to develop his own theories of dream interpretation.

Further developments

There have been many developments in dream analysis since the work of Freud and Jung, but their theories on the unconscious and collective unconscious remain central to most of today's beliefs. Most modern interpreters and analysts agree that dreams often represent issues or desires about which the dreamer feels in conflict, and these often appear in disguise or are hidden beneath the surface. Dream analysis can help bring to the surface anxieties and concerns the dreamer may not have fully acknowledged, and can help people to confront emotions or conflicts they may have repressed.

Many dream analysts today believe that your dreams represent conflicts that are present in your life. Dream analysis can help you to understand these anxieties.

why you sleep and dream

People spend about a third of their lives asleep, and a quarter of that time dreaming. During sleep, the metabolism slows, the immune system concentrates on fighting infection and the production of growth hormone increases, not only for growth but also for repair of body tissue. On a mental level, sleep deprivation leads to poor concentration, memory failure and irritability.

Sleep Patterns

The sleep cycle is broken up into several distinct phases. The first is a period of "slow-wave" sleep, when brain activity, breathing and heart rate all slow down. Slow-wave sleep goes through four stages, the last of which is the deepest, when the brain waves are slowest. This is the time when it is most difficult to rouse someone. After about 90 minutes, Rapid Eye Movement (REM) sleep begins, when the most vivid dreams occur. Phases of REM sleep recur four or five times during the night, between periods of slow-wave sleep. Each REM phase is longer and more intense, from 15 minutes for the first up to 45 minutes for the last, which is often in the final hour of sleep before you wake up.

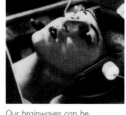

Our brainwaves can be monitored during sleep.

Why You Dream

Studies have shown that if people are deprived of REM sleep they become irritable and lack concentration. They try to catch up on dreams as soon as they are allowed to sleep again by dreaming more than usual, even if this means having less non-REM sleep. This suggests that dreams are in some way necessary for mental and emotional health. They may be a sign that the brain is "ticking over", continuing to interpret signals from the outside world. They may be a form of wish-fulfilment or a way of expressing and resolving emotional crises. Dreams may also be a way for the brain to sort information it has received during the day, as well as considering ideas and grappling with problems.

When You Dream

It was once thought that dreams occurred only during REM sleep, but research has found that dreams occur throughout the night during periods of non-REM sleep, although they are less vivid and are usually forgotten. In the lighter phases of sleep (stages one and two), dreams resemble the fleeting images and thoughts you may experience if you simply allow your mind to drift while awake. Dreams from deeper sleep (stages three and four) are often fragmentary sensations, feelings and thoughts rather than images. When people are stirred from these deeper stages of slow-wave sleep they are often groggy, confused and unable to remember what they have dreamed. In contrast, dreams during REM sleep have characters and storylines played out in a series of vivid images. You will usually wake from REM sleep fully conscious and with clear memories of your dreams.

The body also responds to different types of dream experience. During slow-wave sleep you may twitch, talk or even sleepwalk, but during REM sleep you are virtually still. Although the brain remains active, muscle tone is lost, resulting in virtual paralysis. This means there is no danger of physically acting out a dream, and also explains the sense of paralysis often experienced during a nightmare.

Why You Forget Your Dreams

Even though everyone has periods of REM sleep, some people claim never to dream. This is simply because they don't remember them. But if dreams are important, why is this?

About a quarter of sleeping time is taken up with dreaming, approximately two hours a night. That is a lot to remember, especially if you recall your dreams only when you wake up during them or immediately afterwards. Most people lead busy lives, and wake up ready to get on with the day. Taking the time to think about what you were dreaming of during the night would seem a luxury.

Dreams are also difficult to remember – frequently chaotic and confusing, they flash incoherently from one image to the next. Memories of them tend to be partial and imprecise, and it is always easier to remember dreams that are dramatic and colourful or those that have some personal significance.

During REM sleep the brain is active but the body lies quite still.

preparing to sleep and dream

A peaceful night's sleep will create an environment in which dreams can flourish. Make going to bed a pleasurable ritual, a time when you can put the day behind you and concentrate on the relaxing night ahead. If you are in the habit of going to bed late, retire earlier. The natural human sleep pattern is to sleep early and wake early, so don't stay up late "pottering" or watching television.

Relaxation Techniques

Think of your bedroom as a restful haven in your home where you can get away from the stresses of the day. Don't put computers or piles of work in the bedroom. Keep colours and lighting soft and warm, and tidy away discarded clothes and other clutter.

Relaxing essential oils will help you sleep well.

A long soak in a warm bath has a soothing effect on the body, and can be further enhanced by adding aromatherapy oils. Essential oils are concentrated, so add no more than 5–10 drops to a full bathtub (no more than two drops for children) and consult your doctor if you are pregnant. Experiment until you find the fragrances that work for you, but three oils are traditionally considered the best for sleep. Lavender helps with insomnia, tension and tiredness; sandalwood is purifying, warming and soothing; and jasmine is a balancing oil which helps to relieve stress. Bathing by candlelight will also make the occasion more relaxing and special.

Massage a few drops of lavender or chamomile oil into the soles of your feet before going to bed, as both of these will act as a sedative. Putting a few drops of lavender oil on your pillow will also help to induce sleep.

Avoid caffeine drinks such as coffee and tea at least an hour before retiring as they will probably keep you awake. Instead, have a bedtime drink such as hot milk with honey, chamomile tea or lemon balm (a good restorative for the nervous system).

Once you are in bed, unwind physically by concentrating on the different parts of your body in turn, from your toes to your head. Think about each part and make sure that it is relaxed before you move on to the next: "I relax my toes, my toes are completely relaxed. I relax my calves, my calves are completely relaxed. I relax my thighs... I relax my hands... I relax my jaw... I relax my face..." and so on. Alternatively, first tense and then release each group of muscles, starting at your toes and moving upwards through your calves, thighs, hands, arms, bottom, stomach, neck and face, giving your mouth, eyes, cheeks and eyebrows separate attention.

Finally, if you do sometimes have trouble dropping off to sleep, try not to worry about the amount of sleep you are getting; your body will eventually make sure that you get all the sleep you need. However, if you have persistent symptoms of insomnia, consult your doctor.

Preparing to Dream

Before switching off the light, tell yourself that you will relax in body and mind, go to sleep quickly and sleep uninterrupted through to the morning. Or simply repeat to yourself, "I will remember my dreams." Say this as an affirmation, a positive and gentle way of telling yourself that you feel in control.

Just as essential oils can help you to relax, certain herbs are thought to be conducive to dreaming. The following herbs can be put in a small sachet and kept under your pillow. Mugwort is said to aid dream recall and also to induce prophetic dreams. Rose has a relaxing smell and, like mugwort, is supposed to bring prophetic dreams – especially those of a romantic nature. Rosemary is useful for warding off nightmares and bringing restful sleep; it is also said to be effective if you want a particular question answered in a dream.

Finally, hang a "dream-catcher" above your bed. Originating from Native American culture, this is a net woven on a round frame which is usually decorated with beads and feathers. The net is thought to catch bad dreams, which evaporate with the first rays of the morning sun, while the good dreams drift down on to the sleeper below.

Gentle preparation for sleep reduces the likelihood of insomnia.

analysing dreams

You cannot begin to understand your dreams until you remember them. One of the most effective ways to achieve this is to keep a dream diary. Over time, you will find that you begin to gain an insight into your dream world, and into some of the events that influence your life. You will also become more familiar with the images of your unconscious mind and will begin to recognize and understand your own symbols.

Keeping a Dream Diary

Buy a notebook specifically for the purpose and keep it, with a pen, by your bed at all times. This means that even if you wake up in the middle of the night, you can scribble down your recollections of your dream, or dreams, immediately. It might also be useful to keep a torch by your bed.

As soon as you wake up and before you start writing, close your eyes for a few seconds and try to recapture some of the images in your dream. Most dreams are a series of images and remembering one could trigger the recollection of a sequence. If you can't recall any images, try to remember how you were feeling as this, too, could trigger a fragment of a dream.

Now start writing. You could use the left-hand page of the notebook to record the dream, and the right-hand page for your subsequent notes and comments. It is essential that you write your dream diary before you do anything else in the morning, so try to make it a habit. The more conscious you are in waking life, the less conscious you will be of your dream world, and any activity, such as having a shower or making a cup of coffee, will break your concentration and dissipate the dream. Try to include as much detail as possible, even the parts which don't seem to be relevant or don't make sense to you. Writing in the present tense will make the dream seem more immediate.

In dreams objects may be transformed, yet still strangely familiar.

Once the bare bones of the dream have been recorded, you can begin to flesh them out. One approach is to look at the dream in categories. For example, you could analyse it under the following headings:

Significance: Is there a direct link between the dream and the day's events? Or does the dream reflect something from your past life?

Theme: Did the dream have a main theme running through it? Were you running away? Is it a recurring dream?

Setting: Where did the dream take place?

People: List the cast of characters.

Feelings: Make a note of any emotions you experienced in the dream. Were you angry, scared or frustrated?

Symbols: Did any objects figure prominently, such as a bird, a tree or a train?

Words or phrases: Did any words or phrases in the dream jump out, or seem to have particular significance?

Other notes: Was a particular colour, time of day or season important in your dream?

Sometimes dreaming of a problem may force you to confront it.

Both flying and falling are very commonly the subject of dreams.

Methods of Analysis

Once you have started your dream diary, you will have the material at hand for analysis. Remember to leave space on the pages for this. The longer you keep a dream diary, the more you will be able to make associations. Do certain objects make a regular appearance? Do you have a certain type of dream in times of stress? Are there any patterns to your dreams?

The first step is to decide whether a dream is worth studying more closely. Is it simply throwing up an event from the day before which is neither interesting or useful? Or does it have some greater resonance, a feeling that stays with you or an event that seems important? You could assess it by looking at some of the categories you have already used in your diary:

Setting: Is the place in your dream somewhere you have been to recently, or in the past? How does it make you feel? Try to think of words to describe it. For example, if you dreamt you were back at school, the words might be "young, teacher, learning, test". If you dream you are being tested, perhaps you feel pressurized when you are awake?

People: Are they people you know? If so, what role do they play in your life? Or are they figures you have not met before? Again, try to think of words to describe them. For example, you may have dreamt of a child, whom you describe as "young, sweet, helpless, crying". Does this say anything about how you are feeling at the moment? Do you long to return to your childhood? Or do you feel vulnerable in your waking life?

Feelings: How did you feel during your dream? How did you feel after it? Have you felt a lot like this recently? For example, have you been angry, frustrated or stressed? Emotions expressed in dreams can give you clues about your emotional state when you are awake.

Exploring Symbols

The best way to try to unravel a dream is to explore and interpret the symbols within it. You will be bombarded by images, so try to select symbolic ones that seem important and leave a lasting impression. Symbols can appear in many forms and guises – not just as objects but as people, colours, numbers, even words. Some of the following techniques may be useful in trying to decipher what your symbols mean to you.

Look up the definition of a word in a dictionary. This will sometimes trigger associations that you have not previously considered. There are also plenty of dream dictionaries to choose from and they will give you some idea of what your symbols mean, or could lead to other ideas. Don't take their meanings as definitive, as symbols can mean different things to different people. Drawing the images that have been prominent in a dream can give you fresh insights, or you could try explaining your dream to someone else: putting a dream into words can bring out different aspects, and the person you are recounting it to may contribute ideas of their own

Look at myths, folklore or fairy tales. Some symbols, such as snake, witch and dragon, are dominant in stories. Perhaps a symbol you have dreamt of has played a role in a story or myth, which may give you a new insight.

Free association was the method favoured by Sigmund Freud for dream interpretation. Think of the symbol, then allow your mind to wander through any words that come into your head and see where the train of thought takes you. Carl Jung used direct association. He believed that thoughts and associations should always refer directly back to the symbol. Think of a symbol then, holding it in your mind, write down all the associated ideas and images that come to you. You will find that certain themes recur and certain symbols become familiar. In time, you will learn to understand your own dream language.

Describing a dream to someone else may help you to analyse it.

dreamworking

dreamworking

Once you learn how to understand and appreciate your dreams, you can use them to help you look at things in a different way, to further your self-development and, if not to solve a problem, then at least make you confront or assess it. Sadly, much of what you dream about is likely to be negative rather than positive. Dreams are often about conflict, but this is not necessarily a bad thing: a dream can often make you confront a problem that you may be avoiding or refusing to acknowledge.

Although some of the content of your dreams may be familiar in many ways, the context can be entirely unfamiliar, with a muddled story presented in a series of surreal circumstances. Most dreams exist on two levels. The surface level is made up of the people, events, sights and sounds of the dream. This will probably include fragments from the day – a person you have seen or met, or something you have been thinking about. The second, deeper level holds the meaning of the dream. Not all dreams have meaning – they may be just a regurgitation of images and thoughts from the day. But with time, and by keeping a dream diary, you will be able to identify those that could be interesting or useful to look at.

The most indecipherable, and fascinating, aspect of dreams is the language they use to convey meaning. It is in the form of metaphor and symbol which, like a foreign language, need to be translated and interpreted.

There are a number of theories as to why the unconscious mind should want, or need, to convey information to the conscious mind in symbolic form. One is that the message is something you are not ready to hear, so if it is presented in an incomprehensible way you can easily dismiss it. Freud believed that symbols protect you from the underlying message, which is often so disturbing that it would wake you up if it was presented more clearly. Alternatively, the fact that the message is strange may force you to look at it more closely, and having to decipher and decode a dream could make you feel that you were "solving" a puzzle. Another theory is that you can handle information only in a limited way and that symbols and metaphors are actually an economical way in which to present the information.

Many symbols have been given universal meanings. These meanings are useful as a guideline, as long as you remember that the symbols may mean something different to you. For example, drowning is said to symbolize a fear of being engulfed by an unexpressed need, but maybe you have a fear of water. It is often the feeling attached to it, rather than the symbol itself, that is significant.

controlling your dreams

You can remember and interpret your dreams, but can you control them? To a degree, and with time, practice and patience, you can. Dream incubation involves actively generating a desired dream and has been widely practised throughout history. There are various techniques that will help you to dream about a chosen subject, person or place, to generate ideas, make decisions or simply to have fun.

Psychic Suggestion

Consider carefully what it is you hope to achieve from a dream and write down what you would like to learn from it. Before going to bed, immerse yourself in the subject/person/place you wish to dream about. Look at photographs of the person, think about their character, try and remember times you have shared together, or look at photographs or objects from the place. If you have visited it, try to remember the time you spent there. To dream of a relationship, think about the other person, the times you have shared or the direction in which you want the relationship to go, or how you might change or improve it.

Positive Affirmation

Saying a short, upbeat sentence to yourself can help your mind work in a constructive way. It should be in the present tense and the first person; it should include your name and should be easy to remember. You can use positive affirmation to decide the subject matter of your dream, for example: "I, Jo, will dream tonight about surfing in Cornwall," or to help concentrate your mind on finding the solution to a particular problem. If you are using it for the latter, make sure you focus on the positive outcome and not negatively on the problem itself, for example: "I, Jo, will cope with my workload tomorrow," not "I, Jo, will not get stressed out and feel under pressure tomorrow."

Your affirmation sentence can be written down or spoken. Repeat it regularly during the day, and in bed repeat it to yourself to the rhythm of your breathing.

Study a photograph of a place you want to dream about.

Visualizing Dreams

Visualization is a form of daydreaming that can help bring about a desired mental state. Once you are in bed and feeling relaxed, empty your mind. Now, think as clearly as you can about the end result you wish to achieve from your dream, such as the solution to a practical problem or relationship dilemma. Now try to picture in your mind how you would behave and feel if the problem was resolved – relaxed, more confident and less anxious. Try to be as detailed as possible in your imaginings, then let your unconscious mind mull it over while you are asleep.

Dream Meetings

It is possible to share a dream experience with a friend or partner. Most people practised in the art of mutual dreaming, aspire actually to meet in their dreams. People who are emotionally close usually have the best results, as they often share many of their waking experiences, which can provide them with the dream's subject matter.

Choose a mutual destination that is familiar to both of you. Visualize the scene and describe it to your dream partner in as much detail as possible. Set a time to meet. Be very specific about the arrangements and rehearse them a few times before you go to sleep. In the morning, tell each other your dreams as soon as possible. Sometimes comparisons will not be immediately obvious, for example if you both dreamt in symbols, you will need to decipher the meanings first to see if they compare.

The most important thing is patience – if you don't succeed at first, try again. It is obviously easiest to compare notes if you share a bed with your dream partner.

Looking at a photograph of someone can help you dream of them.

Lucid Dreaming

A lucid dream is one in which the dreamer is aware that he or she is dreaming. Experienced lucid dreamers can consciously manipulate the dream's content – they can think and reason, make decisions and act on them. Not everybody can have lucid dreams easily, but it is possible to learn.

The term "lucid dreaming" was first coined by the Dutch physician Frederik Van Eeden, who began to study his own dreams in 1896. It has only been accepted and studied relatively recently, after dream researchers discovered solid evidence that lucid dreamers not only dream vividly but are also aware that they are dreaming.

Lucid dreamers are usually alerted to the fact that they are dreaming by an illogical or inaccurate trigger: for example, bumping into someone they know to be dead, or flying from a tall building. Sometimes it can be an emotional trigger such as fear or anxiety. Nightmares often lead to a period of lucidity: that fleeting sense of relief when you realize that the horrible scenario you are experiencing is just a dream.

Is there any point in being able to dream lucidly? Tibetan Buddhists believe that lucid dreams are a way of preparing for the afterlife, an environment similar to the dream world. Some masters of Tibetan yoga are said to be able to pass in and out of sleep without even losing consciousness.

A high proportion of ordinary dreams (some people have estimated it as high as two-thirds) have unpleasant elements. They may involve being attacked or chased, or falling from heights, and make you feel scared, anxious or miserable. Lucid dreams, however, rarely focus on unpleasant events. If a dream is frightening, lucid dreamers can detach themselves with the thought, "This is only a dream."

If you are aware that you are dreaming, you could, in theory, be able to change the course of the dream's events. You could decide where you wanted to go, what you wanted to do and who you wanted to meet. You could even decide to confront fears, for example to face the monster chasing you rather than run away from it. Or you could just decide to entertain yourself.

If you want to develop lucid dreaming, you first have to be able to recognize that you are dreaming. There are certain things you can do to help raise this awareness. First, ask yourself the question "Am I dreaming?" while you are awake during the day and just before you go to bed. This will make the question a constant presence in your thoughts. Check the physical reality around you. Is there anything strange or surreal about your surroundings? Can you float above the ground? Have you shrunk in size? The idea is that you make the same checks while you are asleep, and so come to realize when events are in a dream.

Try to maintain a level of mental alertness while falling asleep. Stephen LaBerge, the Director of the Lucidity Institute in California, suggests counting sheep or reciting the 12 times table. This should enable you to remain aware during the transition between wakefulness and sleep, with the aim that at some point you will become aware that you are dreaming. Repeat a positive affirmation before you go to sleep, such as "Tonight I will be consciously aware that I am dreaming."

There is an element of control with lucid dreaming, but you will still be restricted by your own expectations and limitations. You can direct the dream to a certain extent, but you cannot completely control it. For example, once you know you are dreaming, you might decide to visit a tropical island, but you won't know what it is like until you get there. On the whole, dreamers have to accept the basic scenario or concept of a dream, allowing it to evolve while exercising some control over their own actions or reactions. Exerting too much control could also wake you up.

Your ultimate aim could be to meet your partner in a dream.

nightmares

Bad dreams are, sadly, the ones everyone tends to remember the most. This may have something to do with the fact that most people have them so often. In one study it was found that one in 20 people has a nightmare at least once a week, although others go through their lives relatively unscathed, having very few nightmares. Dreams are more often negative than positive, and anxiety is reported to be the most common dream emotion.

Experiencing a Nightmare

Nightmares are laden with varying degrees of anxiety, from mild worry to blind panic. It is the feeling a nightmare evokes, rather than the dream itself, that is usually the most upsetting part of the experience, and even if you cannot recall the details, this is what informs you that you have just had an unpleasant dream experience. In extreme cases, you may even wake up with physical symptoms such as sweating or a pounding heart.

Causes of Nightmares

Certain physiological factors can trigger bad dreams. Eating rich food before going to bed can lead to indigestion and disturb the quality of your sleep; heavy drinkers who give up alcohol may suffer frightening dreams for a while afterwards; and certain drugs, such as BetaBlockers, can increase their frequency.

The strongest trigger, however, is psychological. If you are worried, concerned or miserable about something during the day, then these feelings will prey on your mind at night. They are reflected in common dream scenarios, which are not so much dramatic as mildly disturbing – sitting an examination; discovering a loved one in the arms of another; being inappropriately dressed at a social gathering, or ignored at a party; running but

A nightmare vision of Hell by Heironymous Bosch.

not being able to move. More dramatic common nightmares include being chased by something or somebody; trying and failing to get somewhere; exams, tests or interviews that go horribly wrong, or for which you are unprepared; experiencing or witnessing violence; being strangled or suffocated; feeling paralysed and unable to move or escape.

Susceptibility to Nightmares

Why is it that some people suffer more often from nightmares than others? Dream studies have suggested that those who are more prone to nightmares are "thin-skinned" – they are sensitive, apprehensive and suffer a high level of tension in their waking lives which is carried over into their dreams.

There also appears to be a link between personality types and the types of nightmares people have. For example, ambitious high-achievers are said to have more fantastic, dramatic nightmares. Women have also been found to be more susceptible to nightmares than men. It is perhaps not surprising that feelings of helplessness, or of being threatened, tend to be rather more common in women's dreams.

Vivid nightmares often produce physical symptoms of anxiety.

Night Terrors

These frightening feelings are caused by a sleep transmission disorder which occurs when the brain switches over from slow-wave sleep but doesn't fully complete the process. They are not really dreams as they don't occur during REM sleep. Neither do they feature strong visual images, but they do provoke very physical reactions which can be alarming. The dreamer will not remember much about the cause of their terror – they will just have a fleeting image in their mind accompanied by feelings of guilt, anxiety or shame.

How to Deal with Nightmares

If stress and anxiety are the main causes of nightmares, it makes sense to try to reduce the stress levels in your life. This is easier said than done, of course, but even practising simple relaxation techniques before going to sleep could help.

The best way to cope with dream fears is to confront them. One method for achieving this is to think through your nightmare when you are awake, and rehearse it step by step. When you come to the nasty bit – when the monster appears, or a chase begins, or an attack looms – instead of running away, turn round and face it. Some therapists go even further and suggest that you not only stay put but actually fight back, either verbally or physically. The idea is that if you rehearse the confrontation in your waking life, you will prompt your memory so that you do the same when it happens in a dream.

Another way to confront the fear would be to re-run it over and over again, recording a description of the dream on tape or writing it down, then listening to or re-reading your account. This works on the premise that by continually confronting your fear you will eventually become familiar with it and therefore weaken

A dream guardian – real or imaginary – could protect you when you are having a nightmare.

its power over you.

Finally, you could appoint a dream guardian for protection. Think of a person or animal (it could be someone you know or simply imaginary), whom you could call upon to help you if you have a bad dream. Then imagine yourself back in the dream and call on your dream guardian for assistance. Tell yourself that the next time you have a bad dream your dream guardian will appear to help and protect you. As you fall asleep, remind yourself that your guardian will be there if needed. This is a particularly useful and comforting technique for children who suffer from nightmares.

Try fighting back instead of running away from the monsters in your dreams.

analysis of two dreams

Dreams are individually and uniquely personal, but there are certain themes and images common to everyone, irrespective of background or culture, which crop up again and again. Such common themes, however, can only really be understood in the context of individual lives. Psychoanalysts and dream therapists often explore the thoughts and feelings of their clients with reference to these archetypal images.

Dream Therapy

Whether you are experiencing troubled dreams which haunt your waking life, have a recurring dream that you would like to dispel, or just want to explore your dreams further, then dream therapy might be helpful to you.

Many schools of psychoanalysis use the study of dreams as part of their clinical practice. The therapy involves the patient talking about their dreams as a means of exploring their unconscious and the thoughts, feelings and issues contained within. The dream is then looked at in relation to the patient's life.

Water in a dream represents the unconscious mind.

On a less complex level, there are some therapists who work solely with dreams. There are also dream workshops, in which techniques for dream analysis are taught. Dream groups have also been set up, to which people bring their own dream material to be worked on by the group as a whole.

The following are accounts of two actual dreams which have been analysed by a psychoanalyst and a dream therapist. Both the therapist and the psychoanalyst were sent the narrative of the dream, together with some details about the dreamer and their situation at the time that they experienced the dream. The analyses draw on archetypal symbols present in the dreams as well as insights into the situations of the dreamers.

Winged turtles may be a symbol of creative potential.

"FLYING TURTLES"

At the time of her dream, Kate was 30 years old and working as an administrator. She was considering giving up her job and changing careers.

Kate is in a shallow pond with a lot of other people. They are in a race to row around the circumference of the pond. She begins the race in a boat, which then disappears and instead she is wading round, with water up to her knees. She feels very detached from the others. There are turtles of all different sizes swimming in the pond. The race has finished and everyone begins to leave the pond and walk up a path, the surface of which is covered with more turtles. Kate treads carefully, trying to avoid stepping on them, but she can feel some of the baby turtles getting crushed under her feet. She feels guilty about hurting them. Then suddenly they begin to grow wings, and fly away.

The Analysis

Water in dreams tends to signify the unconscious mind. Kate begins the race in a boat, which is a convenient way of travelling over water without being disturbed by it. It suggests something to do with her relationship with her unconscious, perhaps not being familiar with it, which is also indicated by the water's shallowness. The race is circular, with no beginning or end, which gives it a sense of futility and drudgery, and she is following the path of others. It is when Kate finds herself without a boat and wading through the water that she begins to feel detached from the other people.

The appearance of the turtles is a significant moment in the dream. As well as any personal significance or association they may have for Kate, turtles have a huge symbolic and mythological significance. In some cultures, they are believed to be divine. They often represent fertility and creativity, and turtles appear in numerous creation myths around the world.

Because of the creative significance of turtles, the dream is no doubt saying something about Kate's creativity, possibly a creative potential which hasn't yet been reached or realized. The turtles are also babies, so are symbolic of new life and potential. The fact that Kate walks on them potentially destroys the seeds of creativity, but they are not all destroyed and instead grow wings and fly away to safety, showing the potential for creative expression.

"THE YELLOW DOG"

Sally, in her late 30s, is a designer in the film industry. At the time of her dream, she was working hard, up against tight deadlines.

Sally is in a wide, tree-lined road with big, red-tiled houses set back from the street by long front gardens. There has been a flood and a fast-flowing torrent is running down the middle of the road. Sally is being swept along by the current. She tries to grab hold of a tree trunk and cling on to it. There are no other people around but there is no sense of her having lost anyone, nor is she trying to catch up with anyone. Suddenly, a large yellow labrador swims along. He holds his paw out in the air, leg out-stretched, and says to her, "Grab hold of me." He has managed to communicate without speaking. She holds on to the dog's paw (he is big, strong and solid) and he gets her to safety, but she doesn't remember how. Next, she is in a bar with people whom she doesn't know in real life but knows in her dream. The dog is still by her side, making sure that she is safe.

The Analysis

The setting represents affluence and stability, and could represent these aspects in Sally's life. The trees that line the road relate to family matters – trees are often linked to the family, hence the family tree. The road symbolizes direction in life. The flood shows that emotions are sweeping through any sense of stability Sally may feel and are causing a huge upheaval. It is always better to go with the flow, but Sally is resisting being swept away and wants to be rescued. Grabbing the tree shows she is trying to feel grounded or "rooted".

The yellow dog represents faithfulness and loyalty, protection and rescue. He could be a real person and he may also represent intellect, as the colour yellow symbolizes intelligence. Perhaps Sally relies on her intellect to rescue her from emotional issues because she doesn't want her feelings to get in the way. Even in a social setting – in the bar – the dog is still there to protect her, indicating that she feels she needs to use the rational part of her personality all the time.

The dreamer is resisting being swept along on a flood of emotion.

Common Dream Themes

Flying or floating: Flying dreams commonly bring a feeling of freedom and exhilaration; they are seldom frightening or unpleasant, and the dreamer often awakes with a sense of optimism. The actual process of flying is usually effortless and the body feels weightless.

Being chased: Being chased in a dream suggests that you are running away from a situation that is threatening or frightening, or simply in danger of dominating the rest of your life. Perhaps there are problems that you are not facing, or obligations that are waiting to be fulfilled.

Falling: Whether it is falling from a cliff, a building or a wall, falling is a universal dream theme with a number of meanings. It may signify feeling out of control or overwhelmed by a situation, such as the loss of a job or a divorce. Falling dreams also reflect a sense of having failed or "fallen down", so maybe you have tried to reach too high in your personal or professional life and fear that you are ready for a fall. Alternatively, the fall could symbolize a fear of "letting go".

Drowning: A dream about drowning could reflect an area in your life in which you are finding it difficult to "keep your head above water". Large bodies of water are generally seen to represent the unconscious, so drowning could symbolize feeling engulfed by repressed, unconscious issues.

Losing teeth: Whether they fall out in one go or slowly crumble, dreaming of losing teeth can be quite alarming, although it is very common. Such a dream may reflect fear of ageing (and loss of sexual attractiveness), fear of losing power and control, or fear of change. Biting or being bitten are obviously symbolic of aggression.

Being unable to move: Being rooted to the spot but desperate to escape is a fairly classic anxiety dream. The physical paralysis could be a reflection of an emotional paralysis – perhaps you feel unable or reluctant to make changes in your life, or to make a decision.

Being naked in public: Nakedness can represent the desire for freedom, or freedom of expression, reverting perhaps to childhood innocence. Being naked in public with others' disapproval could indicate fear of revealing your true self.

The faithful dog reaches out a rescuing paw to save the dreamer.

guide to dream symbols

Dreams use the language of metaphor and symbol to convey their meaning. Sometimes a symbol can be fairly straightforward, at other times it can be completely baffling and nonsensical. Some symbols are universal (for example, the dove as a symbol of peace and the cross as a sign of Christ), but within the context of a dream even these can mean different things to different people.

Interpreting Symbols

The most important factor to bear in mind when analysing the meaning of a dream symbol is the way it relates to your own personal experience. This list of symbols is intended as a springboard for your own specific interpretation. It is selective and by no means definitive – some symbols have just one possible interpretation, while others have a variety of meanings. The list should give guidance and spark off your own ideas. It is possible that, in time, you may even begin to develop your own list of dream symbols. Certain objects, people and situations may recur from time to time in your dreams and you will eventually be able to attach your own meaning or significance to them.

The important thing to remember is that the feeling, tone and setting of a dream, as well as its images and events, all have to be taken into consideration when you are exploring the possible meanings of symbols, and what they mean to you on a personal level.

Accident

Being involved in an accident or crash in a dream could be a straightforward fear of being physically harmed. It may also suggest that you are in a state of anxiety, or even fear, or that you are heading for an emotional "crash" or collision. If the general feeling of the dream is positive, although violent, it could symbolize a part of your life that you are letting go.

Actor/actress

Dreams in which you or other people appear as actors tend to represent the public, rather than private, self. If it is an unpleasant dream about acting, it could refer to a situation or situations in your waking life in which you feel that you are being forced to "put on an act".

Aeroplane

An aeroplane can be a positive symbol of liberation and freedom, particularly if you are the pilot and are able to "rise above" a situation or soar to new heights.

Angel

Traditionally seen as messengers of God, angels symbolize purity and goodness. They are also thought of as protectors and guides.

Avalanche

An avalanche signifies being overwhelmed or fearing disaster. If the avalanche is snow or ice, it may symbolize "frozen" emotions that could be expressed or experienced.

Baby

A baby may represent a new beginning, development or opportunity in your life. It can also represent your own "inner baby", the part of the adult you that is still craving to feel secure and looked after.

Bed

A bed can be a symbol of security, warmth and comfort, maybe even of escaping from the outside world. If a bed appears in a dream about marriage or a relationship, then the state of the bed could be seen as representing the state of the relationship.

Bird

Birds carry a variety of meanings. Their flight represents freedom, and they also have a variety of religious meanings as messengers of the divine or symbols of the soul. They represent the "higher self" in most cultures. Blackbirds, crows, ravens and vultures are traditionally interpreted as omens of death. The dove is a symbol of peace and reconciliation.

Birth

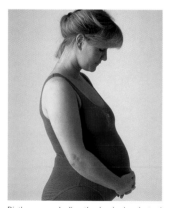

Birth can symbolize the beginning (actual or potential) of a new idea or project, or a sense of beginning a new stage in your life. Pregnant women often dream of difficult or strange births (for example, giving birth to kittens) which could reflect their anxiety about childbirth.

Book

Books represent knowledge and wisdom, or the historical record of the dreamer's life. A dusty old book could symbolize forgotten or neglected knowledge, or an earlier "chapter" of your life. The opening and closing of a book may represent the opening or closing chapter of your life.

Bride/Bridegroom

Weddings can symbolize the union of opposite yet complementary parts of yourself, the most obvious being the union of the masculine and feminine parts of your personality. In Jungian psychology, images of a bride or groom represent the *anima* (feminine traits repressed in the male) in men, and the *animus* (masculine traits repressed in the female) in women.

Car

A car usually represents yourself and, in particular, whether or not you feel in control of your life. If you are in the driver's seat, this may symbolize that you are taking charge of your life. If someone else is driving, you could feel over-dependent on others, or allow others control. You may be put in control of a car before you are ready, or even if you cannot drive.

Cat

Cats symbolize the feminine, sexuality, power and prosperity, and have both positive and negative connotations. They can be perceived as fertile and creative, but also "catty". In symbolism derived from folklore, a witch and a black cat generally stand for evil and bad luck.

Chased (being)

A dream about being chased can bring with it feelings of hopelessness and frustration because you feel you cannot escape. It may be worth looking at who is doing the chasing and what they represent. Is it a figure of authority, or something more threatening? Whatever is chasing you could be an aspect of yourself that you are afraid to confront.

Child

A child could symbolize your own "inner child", the part of you that is in need of reassurance or needs to grow up. Dreaming of children can also symbolize a desire to go back to a more innocent, less complicated time in life. Like a baby, a child can also represent the possibility of a new beginning or a new attitude to life.

City

The meaning of a city depends whether you enjoy or dislike the urban environment. In Jungian psychology, the city represents the community, and could represent your relationships with other people. If you are lost in the city, this would probably represent a loss of direction in life. A ruined city may indicate neglected relationships or aims in life.

Clock/Watch

As dream symbols, timepieces such as clocks and watches often reflect anxiety about not being on top of things or being behind schedule.

Death

Dreams about death could express some anxiety about dying but, symbolically, death represents not so much an ending as a new beginning, so to dream of your own death could mean that you are preparing to start something new. If you dream of the death of a loved one, you may be rehearsing the actual event and unconsciously preparing for bereavement.

Dog

Animals signify the natural, instinctive and animal self. As domestic pets, dogs have a wide variety of symbolic meanings, including loyalty and companionship, going along with the pack and tamed wildness.

Door/Doorway

The meaning of a door or doorway depends entirely on how it appears in the dream. An open door could represent a new opportunity or phase in life, and going through the door would be to grasp that opportunity. Too many doors could suggest that a choice needs to be made. If the door is locked, it may indicate that something is being repressed or hidden.

Drowning

A dream about drowning could reflect an area in your life in which you are finding it difficult to keep your head above water. Water represents the unconscious and drowning could symbolize being engulfed. It is also a symbol for the emotions, and dreams about drowning can happen during an emotional crisis or if you are feeling overwhelmed by your feelings.

Falling

Psychologists have speculated that fearful falling dreams are rooted in early childhood, when you learn to take your first steps. Some scientists have offered a physiological explanation – that your muscles relax as you fall asleep and the falling sensation is the result of an involuntary muscle spasm, which becomes incorporated into a dream.

Fire

This element is a complex symbol meaning many different things, including passion, anger, illumination and danger. Fire can purge as well as consume, purify as well as destroy. An out-of-control fire in a dream could be a sign of unbridled passion or ambition.

Fish

Large areas of water represent the unconscious, so any creature living in water can represent a message or insight from the unconscious. Fish explore the depths of the ocean and are therefore positive symbols for anyone wanting to explore their own depths.

Flower

The flower is a natural symbol of beauty, fragility, harmlessness and the attraction of bees to nectar. In Asian yoga teachings, flowers represent the psychic centres, or chakras, on which to focus meditation.

Flying or Floating

One of the most common explanations of a flying dream is that it represents an ability to cope with life, rising above it and viewing it from an objective standpoint. It could also indicate a love of risk-taking and adventure. If you are flying in a bed or an armchair (or even on a carpet), this suggests a desire for adventure but within the confines of comfort and security.

Forest

A dark forest is a symbol of the unconscious, so venturing into a forest can be seen as an exploration of the unconscious mind. A forest can also represent a refuge from the demands of everyday life.

Giant

A giant can be a friendly or scary symbol, either helpful and protective or terrifying. Because of its size, a giant could represent something large or overwhelming in the dreamer's life, a gigantic obstacle that needs to be overcome.

Horse

This powerful animal represents noble actions. In general, it is a symbol of humankind's harnessing of the wild forces of nature. If you are riding a horse in your dream, it could indicate that you are in control of your life. It could also represent your own emotional state if the horse is running away with you, or if you are reigning it in in your dream.

Hospital

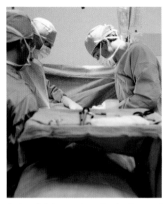

A hospital is a place for healing and getting back into the flow of life. It could also suggest that you may need to pay some attention to your health.

House

A house is usually interpreted as representing the dreamer. The living rooms of the house represent everyday life, the attic represents the higher self, and the cellar represents the unconscious. The state of the house is also relevant. Is it dark and cramped, or light and airy? Is it untidy? Do you get lost in it? Is it undergoing construction? Is it being decorated?

Interviews

Having to undergo an interview in a dream can induce the same feelings of anxiety as sitting an examination. The people on an interview panel could represent aspects of the dreamer, suggesting self-dissatisfaction or judgement.

Island

Finding yourself on an island in a dream may mean that you need peace and solitude. It could also suggest that you are afraid of venturing into your unconscious mind (represented by the surrounding water) and prefer to stay on firm ground.

Mirror

A classic identity crisis dream is one in which you look into a mirror and see someone else's face. The reflection may give you a clue to the nature of the identity problem. A cracked or clouded mirror reflects the distorted face (or image) you may be presenting to the world.

Monster

The appearance of a monster in a dream is usually caused by repressed emotions and fears. It could also represent a part of your personality that you consider unpleasant or ugly.

Mother

Symbolically, a mother represents giving life, love and nourishment. Being the mother in a dream denotes taking care of yourself or of a significant relationship in your life. The meaning of a dream about your own mother would depend entirely on your relationship with her, although the dream could be telling you something about that relationship.

Mountain

Climbing a mountain and reaching the top could be a symbol of achieving your goals in life. Surveying the landscape from the top of a mountain could represent looking at life objectively, or assessing it without emotional attachment. Descending a mountain could mean letting go of insurmountable issues.

Nakedness in Public

The meaning of your own nakedness in dreams depends very much on how it feels to you. If you experience feelings of embarrassment, shame and exposure, then this may reflect problems you have with feeling shy or socially inadequate. If, however, no one seems to notice or care, it could mean that you are happy to reveal your "real self" to others.

Office

If you dream about your own office, this could simply be an indication that you are bringing work home with you and into your dreams. An office can also symbolize authority or your professional position in the world.

Paralyzed

Being rooted to the spot but feeling desperate to escape is a fairly classic anxiety dream. The physical paralysis could be a reflection of an emotional paralysis — perhaps you feel unable or reluctant to make changes in your life, or to make a decision, or maybe you are frustrated about a situation over which you feel you have no control.

River

As with the sea, a river is a large body of water and generally represents emotion. Watching a river flow passively may indicate that life is passing by without enough direction. If the river is bursting its banks, you may feel out of control. Crossing a river by a bridge may symbolize a change in life, or avoiding a flood of passion by observing the water from a safe position.

Road

In dreams, roads represent a direction or goal in life. If the road is straight and narrow, you may feel that you are on the right path. If it is winding or bumpy, your plans may be vague or you may be meeting with unexpected changes or obstacles. If you never get to your destination, something could be preventing you from reaching your goal.

School

A classroom typically represents learning but it can also mean competition or public esteem. Dreaming about being back in the classroom can indicate feelings of inadequacy, especially if the dream centres around unpleasant school experiences. School can also symbolize nostalgia, a desire to relive a feeling of ambition or joy from an earlier stage in life.

Sea

Large bodies of water generally represent the unconscious, so the sea could indicate your emotional state. Are you feeling lost in a small boat, or safe in a large one? Is the water calm or are you overwhelmed by huge waves? Are you afraid of monsters that lurk in the water? It is particularly important to take note of the emotional atmosphere of the dream.

Sex

This is a complex area with a broad range of meanings, depending entirely on the individual. Generally, having sex or seeing others having sex could be a straightforward expression of sexual desire, a desire to bond, or an indication of repressed desires for love. Dreaming about sex with someone "inappropriate" does not necessarily mean you harbour secret desires.

Slope

Trying to ascend a slippery slope is a common dream which suggests that you are failing to progress in a certain area. Stumbling or slipping down the slope may signify that you are forcing yourself to do things which go against your nature.

Station/Airport

Railway stations and airports represent a wide variety of possibilities – a new venture or idea ready to "take off", apprehension or excitement about the future, or a transition in life. They can also be confusing places, so their appearance in a dream may indicate that you need to sit down and sort through a particular problem or conflict.

Stranger

In Freudian terms, meeting a stranger in a dream may symbolize meeting a part of your own unconscious personality.

Teeth (losing)

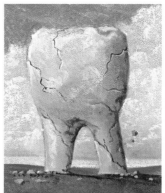

Whether they fall out in one go or slowly crumble, dreaming of losing teeth is very common and slightly alarming. Such a dream may reflect fear of ageing (and loss of sexual attractiveness), fear of losing power and control, or fear of change.

Tests/Examinations

In dreams, examinations can stand for success or (fear of) failure in any area of your personal or professional life. Sitting an examination for which you have not prepared, or in a subject you haven't studied, is a classic fear-of-failure dream. Conversely, passing an exam or test could be seen as a metaphor for having succeeded in something.

Tower

A tower in your dream could be a symbol of caution and vigilance (symbolized by a watchtower) or imprisonment (a guard tower). It could also be an ivory tower, representing arrogance and aloofness.

Train

A missed train could symbolize missed opportunities in life, as could being on the wrong train or missing a stop. Travelling smoothly down the railway track may mean staying "on track" in life. According to Freudian interpretation, the train represents the penis and entering the tunnel (representing the vagina) is a symbol of sexual intercourse.

Violence

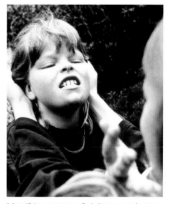

Horrifying scenes of violence or destruction may represent an overwhelming fear of loss of power or control. If you are the one being violent, this could represent a struggle for self-assertion, or a deep-rooted anger and resentment. Directed at you (rather than inflicted by you), violence often represents a sense of guilt and a desire for self-punishment.

mandalas

Mandalas are usually circular in form. In Sanskrit, *mandala* means both "circle" and "centre", denoting that it represents both the visible outer world (the circle) and the interior world of the mind and body (the centre). A mandala is a picture that tells the story of a journey that you can follow from the everyday world to the serene inner centre inside yourself, leading you to a deeper understanding of your relationship with the universe.

Everyone seeks happiness and the fulfilment of their dreams. Mandalas are a tool that can guide you straight to the heart of this search. In following the journey through a mandala you are seeking to find the wholeness that lies at your core, the stillness that always remains no matter what storms may surround you.

When you draw a mandala you can either create an image of your inner self or you can carefully draw out an image of a perfect world and aspire to its expression of harmony. In creating a mandala you open yourself to all the possibilities that exist both inside and outside yourself. You listen to the dreams of your heart, mind and soul and give them shape and colour inside the circle.

A mandala can take any form – seen rightly, any object can transport you from the mundane world to a world of beauty. Once you have begun working with mandalas you may start to perceive the seemingly random reality around you differently, turning what is everyday and commonplace into a journey to your deepest, innermost self.

ancient mandalas

The mandalas of different cultures and different times vary in their form and representation. However, although each may have used a different "language", the mandalas of all ages have described the same cosmos as our own. Irrespective of their historical and cultural origins, if you are able to tune in to their resonance deeply enough, the most ancient mandalas can help you on your journey to finding your own inner truth.

Patterns

Our ancient ancestors saw the pattern of the universe all around them, in the seasons, the waxing and waning moon, and the rising and setting sun. They marked these events with standing stones and circles, and these mandalas now form part of our landscape.

In England, the megalithic monument at Stonehenge heralds the passage of the summer solstice: the complex alignment of stones forms an annual calendar. Our ancestors' way of life was dependent on natural cycles. Stone circles such as Stonehenge are a symbol of their world. Human life is also a natural cycle, and our ancestors built elaborate burial mounds to honour it which also form physical mandalas. Newgrange, in Eire, is a good example. A single ceremonial chamber at the heart of the circular mound lies in darkness until the summer solstice, when at dawn the sun's rays penetrate the passageway, illuminating its dark walls.

The ancient Egyptians also understood the wheel of life. There is a theory that all their pyramids form part of a single pattern on the earth, mirroring the place in the sky where they believed the Pharaoh's spirit would be reborn. At the centre of this vast mandala is a coffin in the King's Chamber. This is the spiritual receptacle for the god's death and rebirth.

The symbolism from these burial places suggests that the centre of the mandala is a place of death and rebirth. We must let the past die in order for the future to open up before us.

The twists and turns of a maze are like a map of the path of life.

Labyrinths

The symbol of the maze occurs in every part of the world, as part of the quest for wisdom and self-knowledge. Each moment you must choose which direction to take, and every wrong decision will make the journey longer. But no matter how tortuous the path you must never lose sight of where you want to be – at the heart of your true self.

In Greek mythology, the story of Theseus and the Minotaur is centred on the legendary labyrinth at the palace of King Minos on Crete. Theseus has to find his way through the maze to confront and kill the monstrous Minotaur in order to claim his destiny as King.

Many simple grass-cut mazes survive from prehistory. They form a single narrow path, which weaves back and forth on itself. Monks and pilgrims would journey through the maze on their knees in deep meditation. These turf-cut mazes demonstrate the simplicity of life when its ever-changing patterns and directions can be accepted with pleasure and peace.

The Celtic triple-spiral maze has many different paths to its centre. Although it is possible to take a short cut through one leaf, in doing so the subtleties of the path are missed. It is only by changing the pattern of turns and not remaining fixed to any single rule that you can pass through the whole maze. It is a reminder that a rich life is one that is not fixated on the future, but relishes the twists and turns of every moment.

The mysterious pyramids were built as the final resting place on earth for the Pharaohs, who were regarded as reincarnations of a god.

Celtic Symbols

The ancient Celts were a diverse people whose influence spread across Europe and possibly as far as Asia. They shared a spiritual heritage of beliefs from the Iron Age to the dawn of Christianity. The Celts developed their understanding of the universe from their ancestors, having close affinities with nature, the seasons, and cycles of life, death and rebirth. Stones decorated with spiral designs and carved round figures, symbols of the earth, are found all across north-west Europe.

The pre-Christian, Celtic cross symbolizes the four seasons and the four directions – north, south, east and west – positioned over a circle of stone, which symbolizes the earth. With the advent of Christianity, the Celts took on elements of the new religion and their crosses became more elaborate. As their skill at stone-carving grew, they carved fantastic monuments with elaborate spirals, animals and mythical creatures from the stories of the saints. These Celtic crosses were inscribed with complete legends and stories which were typically Christian in flavour. A favourite theme, for example, showed the passage of a saint from this life to the next where he would reach enlightenment.

These richly decorated carvings gave rise to the first books – lavishly illustrated bibles which were filled with the symbology of the creatures known to the Celts. Snakes, wolves, fish, peacocks and eagles filled the pages of these illuminated manuscripts along with delicately drawn knotwork. In the Book of Kells, each evangelist was symbolized by his own animal and the decorated borders and letters of the gospels were a richly woven story of the wisdom written on each page. The book was not simply a script but a symbolic journey illuminating a path towards understanding the deeper meaning of the words at the centre.

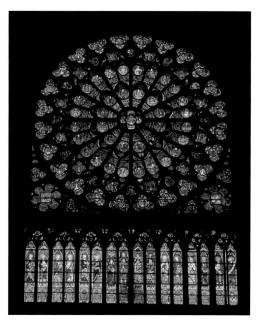

A complex rose window symbolizes wholeness and universality.

Christian Symbols

Churches are traditionally built facing east, in the cross-shape of a mandala. East, where the sun rises, symbolizes the resurrection of the spirit of Jesus at Easter and his gift of new life. The altar is always placed at the eastern end of a church.

The ornate rose windows that adorn cathedrals and churches all over the world are also examples of Christian mandalas. The intricate patterns of stone arches, flowers and vivid colours fill the church with heavenly light and beauty. Sometimes this light spills on to a circular maze on the floor, symbolizing the pilgrim's journey to the spiritual centre of Christianity, Jerusalem.

During the Middle Ages, Hildegard of Bingen had a series of visions that she sought to communicate in music and illustration. She had had a gift for prophecy and vision from her childhood and went on to paint many images describing the world, with man and woman as the pinnacle of God's creation at the centre. In one of her visions she saw God enthroned at the centre of a vast mandala, radiating a circle of gold with a great wheel at his heart, expanding out to encircle the universe.

Hildegard also attempted to describe the harmony of the universe as a path to healing sickness. It was based on her vision of four principal human ailments and the four elements of earth, air, fire and water. She visualized her medicine as an image of the harmonious universe with the elements at the centre surrounded by the wind and the stars. Beyond this lay darkness and fire and the clear light of the sun. At the centre of our true selves, there is no sickness. There we are whole and healed, in harmony with God and the universe.

The intricately carved Celtic cross incorporates both the circle and the centre of a mandala.

native american mandalas   The Native American

people traditionally see all life forms as an integral part of a single existence that surrounds them with its teachings. Every living creature, every rock or stone is part of the pattern of the universe. Everything contains a spirit, which is the essence of its connection with the world. To walk a path of beauty and truth is to walk in harmony with the spirits.

The Medicine Wheel

One of the most important Native American symbols of the universe is the mandala of the medicine wheel. This cross within a circle represents the four seasons (spring, summer, autumn, winter), the four directions (north, south, east, west) and the four elements (fire, water, earth, air), all of which are contained within the outer circle, which is representative of the world. In the two-dimensional wheel, the horizontal axis of the cross also represents the directions of below (Mother Earth) and above (Father Sky). The four seasons are symbolic of time, and the four compass points symbolize space. In addition to these basic concepts, particular animals, colours and qualities invest the medicine wheel with rich and never-ending layers of meaning within the circle that describes the cycle of life.

A Navajo silversmith c. 1870.

According to the symbology of the medicine wheel, when you are born you begin your journey on earth in the east at dawn, a place of light, vision and new beginnings. As you grow up and begin to learn about the world, you move to the south and a time of innocent self-expression and joy. As you grow further you develop your intuition and imagination and suffer the pain of growth in the west. Eventually you move for a time to rest in the north and intuition becomes wisdom. After replenishing your strength, you are ready to begin your journey again in the east, and so the cycle rolls on and turns again, until, after many revolutions of the wheel, you pass into the sky as spirit.

The teaching of the medicine wheel is that you will keep moving around its circumference until you can reside in the centre. Here you become one with the wheel of life and are in harmony with its ever-changing patterns.

The Dream Catcher

The Native American "dream catcher" is a mandala of the dream world. This "wheel" is made from a single thread that is knotted into a spiral web and adorned with birds' feathers and decorative beads. It hangs above a person's head while they sleep and "catches" all the good dreams, whose teaching will remain on waking. The bad dreams, however, pass through the holes in the web and are released into the universe. At the centre of the catcher, the spirit can pass into the dream world.

In a similar manner, Native American shields are created to ensure protection from bad spirits and to act as a call to the person's spirit helpers. Each one of these shields is a unique, individually decorated circle made of skins, feathers, beads and threads. Each one is a weaving of the owner's own spiritual path and is a type of personalized mandala.

A beautiful and extraordinarily large medicine wheel in Sedona, Arizona.

navajo sand paintings

The Navajo believe that illness arises through disharmony with the world. When people do not respect their bodies or the earth, then they become sick. A medicine man (or woman) cures the sick by rebalancing their lives. The healer performs a ceremony, or Way, which is a carefully constructed pathway that brings the patient to a place of wholeness and releases him from his illness.

The Healing Mandala

The Way is centred on a mandala sand painting, the symbol of balance and harmony, and its story. The Navajo call the sand painting iikááh ("the place where the spirits come and go") as they believe that the painting is a doorway through which the spirits will pass as they are called upon in the story.

The healer diagnoses the nature of the patient's imbalance and chooses the most appropriate of hundreds of sand paintings and accompanying myths. The stories that are told are always deeply symbolic, speaking of the creation of the people and the earth and of how humanity has been taught by the spirits to live in harmony with all life.

The medicine man and his helpers begin the ceremony during the day in the hogan, a sacred lodge that has been specially blessed for the ceremony. The sand painting is created using string and other markers to plot the shapes and symbols accurately. The balance and positions of the spirit figures must be exact in order to create a place of harmony for the patient.

The base of the painting is built up using not only sand but ground corn and pollen or crushed petals, and above this, charcoal and ground stone are carefully poured to make the outlines of the figures, with shadows and colours. The figures of the characters in the story are created as solid shapes with the image of their whole bodies, back and front, poured into place to bring their complete presence symbolically into the circle.

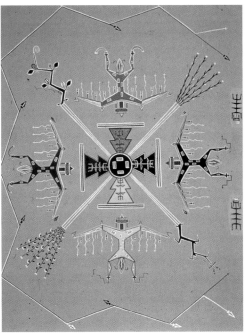

The Navajo healer uses entirely natural materials, including ground corn and petals as well as sand, in the design of the sand painting.

A healing sand painting is created in a specially sanctified lodge.

As night falls when the painting is drawn, the patient, who has not been present at the ceremony until now, comes to the hogan and sits in the centre of the mandala. The images of the spirits are thus in direct contact with the patient so that they may enter his or her body during the ceremony. The healer chants or sings the story of the pathway back to harmony, and while he listens to it, the patient focuses on understanding how he has deviated from his path and in which direction he must walk in future to remain happy, healthy and free.

When the story is told and the patient has heard the lessons and understands the changes he must make in his life, the spirits draw down the illness so that it falls into the mandala. The sand is now infected with the sickness and it is ritually disposed of so that the healed person is free to walk his new path of health.

indian and tibetan mandalas   Traditional

mandalas are a visual meditation tool that helps guide the true seeker to a path of greater understanding of themselves and the universe. Throughout Asia, both Hindus and Buddhists focus on the attainment of wisdom and self-knowledge through meditation, gaining harmony and achieving freedom from the cycle of mortality and the constraints of worldly desire.

Hindu Yantras

Devotees of the Hindu faith use circular yantras in their meditations and ceremonies. Each yantra contains a precisely drawn geometrical symbol of a divinity. Every divine being has its own special symbol of interlocking triangles, pointing up or down depending on whether the deity is of the male or female sex. Surrounding this are circles which symbolize protection and a ring of petals signifying the attendants of the deity. This is all contained within a circular earth-city called *bhu-pura*, enclosed by walls, from which all the guardians of the eight directions sit in a perpetual state of watchfulness.

A beautiful Buddhist mandala.

Yantras can be either a circle, drawn and used flat on the earth, or a pyramid. A round receptacle is placed at the centre, within which the deity will manifest. Yantras can be engraved only on eight so-called tantric surfaces: gold, silver, copper, crystal, birch, bone, hide (which includes paper) and a special stone called *vishnu*. Only these materials, in combination with the use

of the correct colours in the design, will create the balance and harmony of energies for the deity to exist at the centre of the yantra.

Yantras are considered to be alive with the spirit of the deity and must be "given breath" in a ceremony. Scents are smeared over the yantra, while a mantra is intoned over and over again. In the Shri Yantra, letters are drawn around the outside of the circle to symbolize the sound of the creation goddess, Shakti, to whom it is consecrated. When breath and life are given to the yantra it is believed to gain senses to perceive the world and a subtle or spiritual body in which to live. Yantra are sacred objects that can be used as the focus for meditation. In placing themselves at the centre of the yantra devotees aim to become centred in their whole being.

Buddhist Mandalas

Buddhists seek to attain enlightenment so that they can exist in a place of perfect beauty in the universe in this lifetime or the next. The mind and body are taught how to walk in harmony, releasing the person from the constraints of ego and mundane desires. Mandalas are drawn to strict rules to create perfect balance and harmony from which to meditate. There are many paths to enlightenment, and each has its own mandala and its own Buddha to act as guide.

Tibetan Buddhists use the healing and teaching properties of mandalas on a rolled cloth, called a *thang-ka*. These are usually rectangular paintings showing the teachings of the Buddha, the wheel of life, the cosmic tree, saints and other spiritual guides in beautiful, richly coloured images. Tibetans also draw circular mandalas for meditation called *kyil-khor*. Each one contains a wealth of symbols and meaning.

A monk meditates on the mandala by considering each symbol in turn, moving from the edge inwards. The seeker must first pass four outer barriers to enlightenment, which correspond to purifying fire, intellectual strength, the eight states of complete consciousness and the open, innocent heart. They then reach the four gates of the Buddha's palace. In each of the four directions, a protector spirit guards the doorway and must be faced before the seeker can finally enter the palace and reach the mandala centre and the Buddha within.

In a Hindu Yantra, every symbol represents a specific deity.

tibetan sand paintings

Tibetan Buddhists see mandalas all around them. They see themselves as mandalas, they see their country as a mandala and they see all beings, even themselves, as potential Buddhas. The pinnacle of Tibetan mandalas in the physical world is the form of sand painting called *dul-tson-kyil-khor*, or "mandala of coloured powders", and the most complex of these is the Wheel of Time, the Kalachakra.

The Wheel of Time

This path to enlightenment and its mandala describes all the wisdom of the cycles of the universe and the healing that comes from living in harmony with its unceasing rhythms. The Wheel of Time is a two-dimensional representation of a five-storey palace in which the Kalachakra Buddha lives, guarded by 722 divine male and female figures. Each pairing symbolizes one cyclic aspect of the world, and the whole mandala is a single picture of all the cycles in the universe.

The sand painting is seen as only a crude approximation of the true mandala, which as a three-dimensional concept can exist fully only in the mind's eye. The painted mandalas are created to act as aids to help the monks build the mental mandalas, which are necessary in order to follow the meditative ritual texts of Tibetan Buddhism. A monk will mentally walk through all the floors and rooms of the metaphysical palace and seek to pass each figure in turn as part of a meditation, until he reaches the Buddha at the centre and comes to an understanding of the universe moving around him.

The monks begin creating the sand painting with a ceremony to call on the goddess of creation and consecrate the site. They then draw the outline of the mandala on the floor, using white ink and following strict geometrical rules. The painting is created

Once completed, the mandala's role is finished and it is dismantled.

from the centre outwards, symbolizing the creation from a single egg into the universe that culminates in the conscious self. One monk works at each one of the four directions, pouring fine rivulets of coloured sand meticulously from a narrow metal funnel, called a *chak-pur*. For some sand paintings, powdered flowers, herbs, grains and even ground jewels are used to change the spiritual qualities of the mandala.

The palace at the centre of the Wheel of Time is built on the primal energies of the universe: earth, water, fire and wind. The ground floor of the palace contains the cycles of the earth, astronomy and human history. The next storey represents the Tibetan mind-body system of healing. On the third floor is the state of perfection for the human body and mind, which leads finally to the level for the perfect state of being. From this place the monk can truly understand the universe as seen by the Kalachakra Buddha and become one with his state of being.

Creating the Wheel of Time also brings great healing to its surroundings. Once the mandala is finished, its role is complete and a ceremony is performed to release that healing into the world. The sands are swept up from the outside to the centre of the circle and placed in an urn. This is carried ceremonially to a nearby river where it is emptied, carrying the healing sands out into the ocean and around the world to bring peace and harmony to the whole planet.

Coloured sand is poured through a metal funnel in a fine stream.

mandalas of man and nature

You use your senses to experience the world, a world that you are at the heart of. Around you is the air you breathe and the land you walk on. All the time you are awake you can sense the beauty of the whole universe around you. You do not need to go anywhere special to find it. It is always there, waiting for you. In every step you take, you are surrounded by the mandala of the world.

Contemporary Mandalas

In the 20th century, the Swiss psychologist Carl Gustav Jung (1875–1961) developed the use of mandalas as an aid to psychological understanding. He drew a mandala every day to express his innermost thoughts and feelings. Each time he noticed that within the circle he had drawn was a snapshot of his mental, emotional and spiritual state. It was as though the images were reflecting his inner self. He also realized that the expression of the circle was universal – children spontaneously draw them, as do adults when they doodle.

The psychiatrist C. G. Jung.

Jung came to see the mandala as a pathway to the self, and he began to use it in his work as a psychiatrist to help his patients make deeper connections with themselves. The circle or sphere of the mandala represents the psyche that holds within it, at the centre, the true self. He believed that the top of the mandala indicated emotions that were held in the conscious mind, while the base symbolized areas of feelings and thoughts that were deep in the unconscious.

Jung's influence has been far-reaching and today many people are interested in creating mandalas and using them as tools for self-expression. With the spread of many old magical traditions through Western civilization, new mandalas have appeared. The Order of the Golden Dawn is a group that combines Eastern traditions with Western magic. It has created a set of mandalas called Tattva Cards, as an aid to reaching the spiritual self. They contain simple symbols such as moons and circles that are meditated on to develop the vision and experience of the inner self.

Perhaps one of the most exciting forms of the mandala generated in recent times is that of computer art. Three-dimensional computer graphics can bring the realization of a mandala into another digital dimension. The information about the mandala on a computer is stored as a pattern of ones and zeros. This pattern is in itself another representation of the mandala that can be copied and communicated to any other computer throughout the world. Beyond this, all the words we speak into the telephone, all the faxes or e-mails that we send, become pulses of electricity or light radiating around the world in a never-ending stream, an invisible mandala of information, reaching us through television and radio and bouncing off satellites in space, or pulsing beneath the sea along vast cables of light.

The Human Body

Inside your body, your blood, your organs, your muscles, the electricity passing through your nervous system, each tiny part of you, moves and works in harmony with the whole, every single moment that you live, working in unceasing rhythm. When you stand on the earth and reach out with your arms, your silhouette forms a five-pointed star. It is extraordinary in its symmetry and regularity, and is part of the harmony of the universe.

The DNA strands at the centre of every single cell of your body combine to form a map, a blueprint in line with which you develop through life. You are the sum total of your parents and their parents and all their forebears stretching back before them. The genes in your body hold the history of every one of your ancestors, as well as the purity of your heart, mind, body and soul. Without guilt, fear, jealousy and all the other emotions that act as barriers to your true self, you can just be, exactly as your genes describe you. You hold the key to happiness in the centre of every cell of your body.

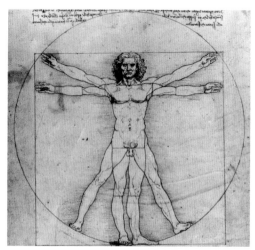

Leonardo da Vinci explored the exquisite geometry of the body.

Mandalas in the Sky

Whether by day or by night, the sky is a source of wonder and fascination. Throughout the year, clouds weave and spin above, forming intriguing patterns. They collect, swell and darken with rain, then part to reveal blue skies. Their patterns reflect the motion of the earth, the oceans and the wind. The flight of a butterfly on one side of the world may influence the weather on the other. Everything in the universe is connected, and the clouds are a reflection of every drop of water, everywhere.

Winter is the season for snow and ice. As moisture drops from the clouds, it freezes and captures in that instant all the motion of the wind and the earth to create a single, unique image – a snowflake. Each one is a picture of the winds and weather everywhere around you.

On a clear night you can see the movement of the stars as they slowly turn around the Pole Star, Polaris, sitting at the tail of the Little Bear constellation, unmoving in the northern sky. It has taken hundreds of years for the light of some and a few years for the light of other stars to reach the earth. In every moment you are looking into a myriad of histories. The canopy of stars spreads out in a vast mandala – a spinning image of space and time.

Mandalas on the Earth

Although it is not generally apparent, we are all living on a huge spinning sphere. As the earth spins, gravity connects you to the very core of the planet, keeping your feet firmly on the ground. You are at the centre of your own mandala. Rivers and oceans encircle you. Mountains, trees and tall buildings stretch above you. Urban or rural, your daily view is full of wonder that can enlighten your soul if you choose to notice.

A single stone is created by all the pressures and motions of the earth. It is formed over thousands of years from minerals and metals or boiled from the earth's crust and cooled over centuries. Water might pound its surface to smoothness or maybe grind it in the waves to form sand. Every stone carries within it an infinitely complex web of creation.

A tree, with its branches reaching out to the sky and roots spreading down into the earth, is a living mandala. Through its size, shape and texture it is a picture of its growing history. It

The constellations revolve around the Pole Star in a huge mandala.

embraces all the moments of its past, both recent and long ago. It indicates when the sun has shone on its branches, turning them upwards, and all the times when rain has soaked into the soil, encouraging its roots downwards. The trunk of a tree shows the same story, formed as a pattern of rings, built up year after year around the centre – the moment of its birth.

The Universal Pattern

There is beauty and truth throughout the cosmos. The food that you eat is full of complex molecules. The person you are today is built from the food you ate yesterday, last month, even last year. Each molecule is a beautiful arrangement of elements, held together in a pattern that your body can read and understand.

When you look at the elements – such as hydrogen and oxygen, which form water – you find that they too are a mandala of little electrons spinning in beautiful, harmonious waves around a centre, a nucleus. Inside the nucleus, you can see that the mandala of the universe is also there. Heavy protons dance a slow stately dance, a pattern from which all the energy of the sun is derived, while inside them little quarks buzz around each other, and so it goes on.

Switching from this intricately detailed, microscopic view of life and looking at the wider, bigger picture, you can see the earth rotating on its axis with humanity on its surface encircling that centre and the moon spinning around it. You can look out at the solar system and all the planets rotating about the sun in an ever-changing pattern. Beyond, you can see our galaxy, rotating as a beautiful spiral mandala about a bright central core. And even beyond this you see the expanding universe enfolding and spreading out into infinity. The universe never ceases. Everything is dancing in a pattern around you.

The symmetry of a spider's web typifies the harmony of nature.

ways of seeing

Looking deeply into the circle of a mandala means that you must look deeply into yourself. It sometimes takes courage to study the picture in front of you and see the storms and turmoil and yet also the peace and beauty that exists within the centre. By studying a mandala in sufficient depth and detail, you can connect with your inner self and look out at the world from the centre of your being.

Looking and Understanding

A mandala may be elegant and intricate, laden with symbols and vibrating with colour, or it may be simple and sparse. Either way it contains its own wisdom and truth. To unlock its secrets you must look below the superficial impression and understand the detail within each tiny aspect of the pattern. If you understand the message of each shape and colour it will help to change you and bring you closer to a place of peace.

This intricate way of seeing, of always looking more deeply into things, brings an original and fresh way of experiencing the world. Look more closely at a tree and you will see the patterns of moss over its bark. Study the moss and you will notice water droplets trapped in its rough surface. This is the way with mandalas. There is always more to see.

You can use this understanding to take action and make changes in your life. If you are in pain for example, you can look and see what is causing it. Perhaps you need to change something that you are doing, or maybe let go of some old hurts from the past. When you see what makes you happy you can alter your course in life to follow that path. Mandalas can tell you without sympathy or restraint, the truth of where you stand, and you can allow that honesty to permeate your life.

Colours

Through your cultural heritage you carry an understanding of the meanings for the colours that fill your life. Although every culture attaches its own meanings to various colours, they are often similar: after all, the sky is blue and the night is black no matter where you are in the world.

Each colour has its own meaning. Red is the colour of blood and life, and of the pain and passion which comes with the initiation of change. Orange signifies bright beginnings and the determination to move forwards into the light and away from the dark. Yellow conveys the need for motion, where you are almost there at the whirling centre, but have slipped and become stuck. Green stands for growth and harmony. It is the colour of innocence and joy when something new is beginning to form. Blue is a place of stillness and inner strength, from which you can express your dreams. Purple expresses the transformation of the past and faith and knowledge in your own inner centre.

The tiniest patch of moss holds thousands of water droplets.

The Rainbow

The rainbow is an especially beautiful colour symbol. Red, orange, yellow, green, blue, indigo and violet arranged in sequence, together make up the colour spectrum. It literally contains all the colours under the sun, without which there would be no life. It is created by the elements of fire and water – the rainwater in the air refracts the fire of the sun. It is a symbol of wholeness and hope, arching through the sky with the fabled pot of gold always at its end on the earth.

Chakras

In the East, Buddhists and Hindus believe that the body has seven energy centres, called chakras, that govern the health of the spiritual, mental and physical being. When healthy, these points are like spinning whirlpools of energy, circles of life. They are connected in a line that runs up from the base of the spine to the top of the head. Each chakra is responsible for a different area of life and is associated with a different colour.

Base chakra (blood red)
This centre is at the end of the spine. It is connected with passion and the primal energies for survival.
Navel chakra (orange)
This centre governs self-worth and self-belief.
Solar plexus chakra (yellow)
This symbolizes self-awareness and independence of being.
Heart chakra (green)
This is associated with taking responsibility for yourself and the ability to give and receive love unconditionally.
Throat chakra (light blue)
This centre represents honest self-expression and giving your talents to the world.
Third eye chakra (deep blue)
This is positioned between the eyes, where intuition, imagination and spiritual awareness sit.
Crown chakra (purple)
Positioned on top of the head, this represents your connection with the universe and the centre of your whole being.

Shapes

The everyday shapes that you see around you, or that you inscribe in a mandala, all have meaning and relevance if you choose to see it. When you look down at your drawing, trust your intuition about the shapes that you see. Always believe what your inner voice is saying and not what another person tells you. Basic shapes also have traditional meanings.

Circle: These are a symbol of wholeness and eternity. The inner circle of the mandala represents the most profound part of yourself. Its ring forms a barrier to what lies beyond, protecting something which is extremely precious and vulnerable.

Line: A single line can be straight and hard or curled and soft. It can be short and determined or long and sinuous. Hard lines often represent repression and pain. Softer lines may indicate indecision and lack of motion.

Cross: Two intersecting lines symbolize the crossing of two forces within you. They may be equally balanced if the cross is symmetrical or they may be antagonistic where one is dominating the other. The centre of the cross on the medicine wheel is the point of balance in a harmonious inner world.

Spiral: This is an ancient symbol of the womb. The spiral is a line that takes you from the broad sweeps of the outer life to an infinitely small centre where you cease to exist. It is therefore a symbol of change and rebirth into something new.

Crescent: This symbol is associated with the moon, which may be waxing and growing in strength or waning, symbolizing loss of power. It speaks of unconscious and instinctive powers.

Triangle: The three sides represent three aspects of yourself – mind, body and spirit. Together they interact and form a whole and may move you on to something new, in whichever direction they are pointing.

Square: The four sides of a square represent stability and security, the solid foundation of your personality and inner strength.

Star: These are brilliant signs of hope. Whether tiny specks or large brilliant objects, when times are dark they can remind you of the light within you and encourage you not to give up.

The changing moon reflects the rhythms and cycles of life on earth.

Numbers

The number of objects, the number of colours and the number of segments you use to divide up the mandala may all have significance, as numbers have their own symbolism.

One: The universe and eternity. One represents the uniqueness of every individual and every moment that you breathe. At any time, in any instant, you can change your life and be centred and at peace.

Two: Opposition and balance, equals and decisions. Night and day, sun and moon, each exists in harmony with the other. Two is the link between opposites where you must decide which path to take.

Three: The eternal balance between life, death and rebirth. It represents the whole self, physical, mental and spiritual.

Four: Change and cycles. It is shown on the medicine wheel by the four seasons and the four compass directions. You must always be moving with the wheel of life, letting the rhythm of its cycles flow through you and carry you on.

Five: The centre of the wheel, the fifth point in the circle of four directions. You have five fingers and five senses to interact with the world and when you stand, grounded with your legs apart, your body forms a five-pointed star. Five is the number of connection with the earth, the sky and the present moment.

Six: The four directions, north, south, east and west, plus the two opposites, earth and sky. Six is often connected with feminine energies and imagination, the "sixth sense".

Seven: The heavens, the sky, and the days of the week. There are seven colours of the rainbow, seven notes in the musical scale, seven chakras in the body, and seven visible planets. In a mandala it is the number of universal harmony.

Eight: Perfect balance. The eight-spoked Dharma wheel of consciousness in a traditional Buddhist mandala leads to a state of awareness which is perfectly balanced.

Nine: Deep wisdom and knowledge. A mystical number that represents the merging of the spiritual, mental and physical.

Ten: Completion. It is a sign of learning that allows you to be reborn into something new and different. It is often regarded as a number of perfection and balance.

The light and colour of nature can inspire new ways of seeing.

mandala meditation

A mandala is a picture of wholeness and harmony. It has been created from a place of wisdom and contains the essence of wisdom at its centre. Consequently, it is a powerful meditation tool which can help to restore a sense of inner strength and peace. You can use any mandala for your meditation – anything from a traditional Buddhist mandala to one created entirely by yourself.

An Inner Mandala

Place the mandala you have chosen for your meditation before you, preferably hanging on a wall in front of you rather than lying on the floor. Make sure it is well lit with natural or natural-coloured light so that you can see it clearly. Kneel with your back straight, your head up, and your hands resting comfortably in your lap. Close your mouth and breathe through your nose. Close your eyes. Count ten slow breaths and let your mind become still.

Now open your eyes and focus on the edge of the circle, noticing all the shapes and colours and what they mean to you. Move your eyes closer to the centre and look at all the intricate patterns of the mandala. Once you have looked at something, let it go from your mind and move on to the next pattern. Continue moving inwards, seeing and understanding all there is to see, until you reach the centre. Now focus on that smallest point at the centre of the mandala, and let your mind become still once more. Close your eyes and follow the entire journey again in your mind's eye,

Soft candlelight may help you to look more deeply.

starting at the outer wall of the mandala and moving in to the centre. See what you can remember of the experience, what you felt was important to you, and let the rest be forgotten. Don't struggle trying to remember every single detail. Paint the mandala as you recall it in your mind's eye and see its patterns and shapes inside you.

When you feel ready, mentally place your inner mandala in a special place. This could be somewhere inside you, such as in your heart, or in an imaginary place such as a golden casket, or in a favourite spot you know in nature. You can go back to this special place and reach that mandala whenever you want to meditate on it again or to be reminded of its beauty and peace.

Meditation for the Inner Self

First make the room into a meditation room by lighting candles, incense, playing soft and relaxing music and making sure that you have somewhere comfortable to sit.

To see into all the depth and subtlety of an inner mandala you must become quiet and still within yourself. Simple breathing and meditation exercises will quieten your mind and allow the voice at your centre to speak clearly. Place the mandala in front of you so that you can see it clearly. Kneel with your back straight and your head up. Relax, close your eyes, breathe slowly through your nose and take ten slow breaths to still your mind.

Open your eyes and gaze at the mandala. Let parts of it attract you and see what they remind you of. Notice shapes, patterns and colours. See what is at the edge and what is at the centre. Defocusing your eyes slightly may help you see more deeply into the mandala and allow it to "speak to you". Sit and gaze, letting thoughts triggered by the mandala rise and fall, all the time remaining focused on the painting. Spend five minutes or more on this meditation.

Once you feel you have seen everything, close your eyes and remember for a moment those parts of the mandala that held the strongest attraction for you. Did those parts have any particular messages for you about your life? If so, what can you do now to affect changes in your life in the light of that new knowledge? When you open your eyes have in mind one action that you will do in response to listening to your inner voice.

Burn incense in your room to prepare it for meditation.

healing with mandalas

Mandalas interact with the centre of your being and from this pivotal point you can affect great changes that will bring you to a place of health, happiness and harmony with the world. If you change the way you think, you can change the pattern of your whole life. If you follow the Navajo and Native American belief that all illness begins in the mind, by changing the way you think you can also remain healthy.

Acceptance

If you do fall sick, you can at least work to improve your mental attitude. Whether you are suffering from a mental, physical or spiritual illness, mandalas can help you focus on accepting the pain or sickness as a first step to letting it go and returning to health.

Find some quiet time to focus on your self. First lie down, with your hands by your sides, and breathe slowly. Focus on the pain or sickness inside you. Let it rise to the surface of your mind and body. Now sit and draw an inner mandala of that pain, expressing your inner self spontaneously on paper in any way you feel is right. Let every emotion and feeling that you have associated with the illness be expressed in the circle. Be true to your pain. If you feel despair try to give the feeling shape and colour in your drawing. If you have flu, for example, imagine what this "looks" like and express it wholeheartedly.

Listening

Sit quietly and focus on your mandala using the Meditation for the Inner Self described opposite. Consider carefully each symbol that you see and what it means to you. Think about your habits and what thoughts and actions may have helped to develop the

Use a natural object, such as a leaf, as a symbol of change.

illness. What can you do differently from now on? Pick a single change that you can make in your life which will lessen the chances of the sickness or pain recurring. For example, you may be able to think of a new way of behaving in your job that could reduce your stress levels and susceptibility to flu.

Releasing

Use meditation to contact a place of peace and hope inside yourself. Imagine a symbol that represents the change you have decided to try. This could be a tree, an egg or a rainbow for example, but it should have meaning and feel right for you. Paint or draw the symbol into a mandala, using all the positive intention you can muster. In this way you are physically working towards making the change in your life. Now meditate on the mandala and hold it in your mind's eye. Whenever you have an opportunity to make the change, remember the mandala and all the positive associations that it holds for you.

By making changes inside yourself, you not only affect your own life, but also the lives of the people around you. By bringing yourself to a place of healing you bring a little more health and happiness into the world, and the balance of the planet moves closer to a place of harmony too.

Focus on the beauty and harmony of the natural world to help you consider ways of changing your life for the better.

the centre of the mandala

Mandalas capture a moment in time, embodying it as a circular picture or object. The circle is a potent and universal symbol of wholeness and eternity, and its energy is focused at the centre. At the heart of the mandala is its deepest and most profound point. It is possible to pass this on to others as a gift or to use it to help bring you closer to your own centre of being.

Personal Mandalas

Creating a mandala for yourself allows you to give direct expression to your innermost thoughts and feelings, and to produce an aid to your meditations that will help you to understand yourself in new and deeper ways. A personalized mandala for someone else whom you know well is a very special gift honouring that person's qualities. Spend some time thinking about the person you want to give the mandala to. Meditate as you would for drawing your own inner mandala but think about the recipient rather than yourself. What are their joys and sorrows? Is there a special occasion that you want to honour? What is it about this person that you like? In the circle in your mind, think about the colours which most represent that person and what symbols you associate with your feelings. When you come to create the mandala consider the materials you could use and be creative in your expression of their inner essence.

Widening ripples on a pool are a natural mandala.

Understanding the Universe

You can also create a personal mandala to help bring more understanding and clarity of thought into difficult areas of your life. Is there someone with whom you find it hard to interact? Is there a creature that you fear? What things in life or in the world would you like to understand better?

Everything in the universe can be seen as a mandala, and you can therefore create a symbolic representation of anything that you like. Through making a personal mandala out of the universe around you, you can reach an understanding of any part of the cosmos.

Focus carefully during your meditation on the person, creature or part of the world that you want to understand. In the circle of your mind's eye, pull in patterns and colours that spontaneously come to mind. As you paint them, keep your attention focused on that person, creature or situation. Once you have finished, meditate on that inner circle and see what it tells you. You may see the world from the perspective of the other person or you may recognize some of your feelings about them. Listen to what the mandala says to you and the symbols will help guide you to a new place of understanding.

Changing your Life

By focusing your thoughts on changing an aspect of a mandala, you can focus your thoughts on changing your life. It is through your intent of purpose that you will change the way that you live in the world around you.

What do you dream of achieving? What changes do you need to make in your life to take you closer to your dream? Consider one change that you would like to make. Draw an inner mandala focused on that part of your life the way it is now. Express in your drawing of the mandala what it gives you, as well as what it denies you.

Now put it to one side and draw a second inner mandala. This time focus on your life after the change you are contemplating has occurred. Are you behaving differently? What does this change give you and what does it deny you? By painting the change and by holding the pattern of this second mandala in your mind you are actively seeking to make your new behaviour a reality in your life, and paving the way for it to happen.

Paint a personal mandala as a gift in honour of a close friend.

teachings of the mandala

The mandala teaches that in everyone there is a place of beauty. To live in this place is to be happy, healthy and free. This is the life of your dreams. Everyone has a different dream for their lives, and it is up to you to realize what is unfulfilled at your centre and begin to make the changes in your life that will enable you to be content and live at the centre of your dream.

Finding Truth

Mandalas are one of many tools that you can use to guide you to your centre and to find what burns at the heart of you. No matter which method you use, all require the deepest level of self-honesty. Speak your truth. Speak it loudly to yourself and louder still to everyone around you. It does not matter if no one else believes you. If you know in your heart that you are following your dream, you can then hold on to that belief and you will reach your goal. You can have anything you want, as long as you are true to your centre and your inner self. Paint a mandala of your dreams, of everything that you want in life. What is the one thing you want to achieve before you die? Paint it and hold it in your mind's eye as a talisman against your own doubts. As you reorient your life towards your centre, paint new mandalas which will reveal more and more about your dreams and perhaps show other new possibilities opening up.

The journey to the truth is not an easy one. In any mandala there are circles of fire to be crossed, and the tombs of old hurts to be unearthed and laid to rest. At the heart of each mandala, however, lies the centre, drawing you on and waiting for you to reach it. Take small steps along the path and slowly but surely you will find that you have crossed the mountain and come to rest in the life you always longed for.

The Buddhist Dharma Wheel, enshrined on a lotus flower and surrounded by sacred flames, represents the eight truths.

Living in Truth

On the road to your dream you will find obstacles. Buddhists use the eight-spoked Dharma Wheel to remind them of the eight precepts of the Buddha that guide them on the right path to fulfil their destiny.

Right Belief This is belief in yourself. You must be sure that you are listening to the true voice of your inner self and not to that of the ego.

Right Resolution This is the intent with which you take the steps on the road to your dream. This should always be approached with humility.

Right Speech These are the words that you speak on your journey to your centre. If you deny your truth, if you dishonour yourself, then you also deny that centre.

Right Action These are the deeds that you do in the pursuit of your dream. If you do not take the necessary action, you can never reach your goal.

Right Living This is a reminder that all your habits, good or bad, can take you closer to or further away from your centre. Right eating, sleeping and exercise can all take you closer to your dream.

Right Effort This is the energy that you use in your life. If the source of your inner energy is blocked, your actions will be half-hearted.

Right Thinking These are the thoughts that fuel your intent. If you think selfishly or with petty emotions then your intentions can never take you to your centre.

Right Peace This is the dream that you hold and the place where you can choose to be.

creating a mandala
creating a mandala

creating a mandala

There are moments in life when you need to stop and look within. These are the times when you are feeling "out of touch" with yourself, when your inner voice has become muffled or simply lost in the business of your everyday life. At these times you need to reconnect with what you truly feel and to find out what it is you really need in order to become happy and healthy again.

The mandala traditions of the Buddhists provide a wealth of imagery and symbolism – beautiful circles con-  taining palaces and diamonds, guardian spirits and lotus leaves. However, the essence of the mandala is translated into every language and culture, in sand paintings, medicine wheels, rose windows, stone circles and even com- puter-generated art. Regardless of time or place, every human being holds the key to unlock their unique path to happiness.

Creating a mandala can help you to find your still centre within. The art of creating a mandala involves turning your attention away from the outside world towards yourself and your inner universe. Every person is unique and each one of us has beautiful qualities. These may be evident or they may be hidden, but they are there all the same. By becoming quiet, by silencing all those loud voices in your head, shedding your endless worries, stilling your endless desires, you can recognize the peace and harmony that exists all around and inside you.

There are two paths that you can follow in creating your own mandala. The first is the more traditional way, which follows certain specific rules and procedures. This is how mandalas are traditionally created throughout the Buddhist world. If you sit and follow the elaborate steps accurately, you will create a picture of the perfect balance you are seeking. In the process of following the intricate rules of mandala-making, you can come a little closer to your inner self. You can keep these traditional man- dalas for when you need to focus on your inner world, or destroy them when they have taken you to where you needed to be.

The second method is more spontaneous, free-flowing and less structured than the traditional approach. In this type the mandala is not planned. It is achieved by picking up a pen and simply drawing. This method is useful for giving you a window into your inner self. Through what you create, you can begin to see where you need to heal. The very act of drawing a mandala may be enough to bring you back to a place of peace and harmony with the world.

buddhist mandala

When you create a traditional mandala, you are working towards making a picture of perfect peace. It is important to start by creating the right space inside and outside yourself. Tibetan monks meditate and fast for three days before embarking on a painting. Although you need not go to such lengths, you can follow some simple steps to open yourself to the stillness and balance that you want to come into your life.

Preparation

Select a suitable place to draw the mandala, where you will be undisturbed and feel at peace. Fill the space with beautiful music or burn incense and candles to create a sense of peace.

Breathe in slowly through your nose. Start with your arms hanging loosely, fingertips touching, then raise your arms outwards and up above your head. Breathe out as you return to the relaxed position. Imagine that breath in as white light filling your lungs. As you breath out imagine that the air you are releasing contains all your worries and anxieties. Let your mind become quiet and still. Imagine that the music or incense is reaching into all the corners of the room and dissolving any dark areas into light. Picture your space bright and clear around you.

Shake your hands to loosen the wrists. Then clench them into a ball and release a few times, feeling the blood and life flow through your hands. Gently massage each finger right to the tip. You will feel your hands almost grow as they become energized.

Sit down and close your eyes. Keep your back straight and your body relaxed. Now you are ready to open your eyes and pick up the compass. Draw the outer circle. Now close your eyes and see it in your mind's eye. Look at the emptiness at its centre and imagine how it will be filled. Think about the journey you are describing, from the mundane world to the peace at the centre of the circle. Feel how close you are to the centre already.

Open your eyes, pick up your pencil and begin.

Focus on the feelings of harmony you want to bring into the space.

Drawing the Mandala

The following steps lead to a simplified Tibetan Buddhist mandala. The geometric rules follow similar patterns to those traditionally used by Buddhist monks, and some traditional symbols are used, although you may find it more helpful to use your own symbols. The mandala can be drawn to any scale.

You will need
- Pair of compasses
- Pencil
- Ruler
- Large sheet of paper
- Coloured pens or paints

1 Mark the mid-point of each of the four directions and then draw four circles from each of those points. Draw two diagonal lines to connect the intersections of these circles and the centre, to form the eight directions.

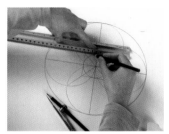

2 Mark the mid-point of each of the four directions of the second cross and draw a small circle to connect them together. This forms the walls of the central palace. Now draw the square to surround that circle.

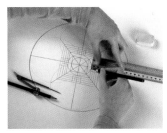

3 From the points where the diagonal lines cross the circumference, draw the square that fills the inner circle, then draw the circle that fills that. This final small circle is the seat of the Buddha at the centre of the mandala.

4 Along each arm of the first cross, mark the mid-point between the palace and the circle edge. Mark the mid-point between this on either side, repeating the subdivision four times. Draw four squares as the foundations of the palace.

5 Mark the mid-point of each half-side of the palace square. Subdivide again towards the centre. Connect the outer marks with the outer foundation of the palace and the inner marks with the next foundation. These are the palace gates.

6 Draw four circles with their centres at the middle of the outer foundation line and their width the distance to the palace. The outer semicircle, beyond the gates, is the area of the spirit that protects entry to the palace.

7 Finally, returning the point of the compass to the centre of the mandala, join the four marks within the circle edge to form four inner circles. These additional circles represent the four barriers to enlightenment.

8 When the drawing is complete, you can considering the colours and symbols you wish to use to fill the mandala. Each traditional colour has many layers of meaning, but use the ones you feel most express the symbolism of your mandala.

Colours and Symbols

The traditional colours used in Tibetan mandalas are white, yellow, red, green and blue, and sometimes gold is also added.

Within the Inner Palace at the centre sits the Buddha, who is both the representation of an enlightened being and of yourself when you are happy, healthy and free. The lotus flower with its eight petals is used by Buddhists to signify this state. The lotus grows in mud yet produces a beautiful flower. It symbolizes how it is possible to remain firmly rooted in the earth and yet reach for the sky.

The four directions within the palace signify the cycles of the earth and time. They are a reminder that the wheel of life is always turning and each step on the wheel can take you closer to the centre.

The foundations of the palace are the primal elements which make up the universe and from which we are all ultimately made. From the palace down, these four tiers are coloured with the yellow of earth, the white of water, the red of fire and the blue of wind.

Protective spirits, or doorkeepers, bar entry to the palace, one in each direction. Only those who approach with pure intent may pass through it. A traditional symbol that marks this space is the eight-spoked Dharma Wheel. Each one of the spokes represents one of the steps on the path to enlightenment, which are right belief, right resolution, right speech, right action, right living, right effort, right thinking and finally right peace.

Finally there are four outer barrier circles, indicating key stages through which you must pass. The outermost of these is a ring of fire, symbolizing the flames of purification which burn away ignorance. Moving in towards the centre of the mandala is a ring of diamonds, indicating light and illumination of the mind as well as the mental strength and endurance needed to reach the centre. Next there is a circle divided into eight burial grounds. These indicate the eight states of consciousness through which you must pass: seeing, hearing, tasting, smelling, body awareness, thinking, self-awareness and basic consciousness. The fourth barrier is a circle of lotus leaves. These symbolize the process of emotional rebirth that you have embarked upon.

native american mandala

The Navajo create sand paintings as part of a healing ceremony. This painting is based on one of a sequence used in a creation myth and ceremony called the Blessingway. The ceremony celebrates the coming into the world of abundance and life, represented by the four sacred crops, tobacco, squash, beans and corn. It is performed to celebrate or bring about a turning point in someone's life.

The Blessingway

The Navajo sand painting is traditionally made from sands or ground powders. However, these authentic ingredients are difficult to obtain. Instead, you can use paints or coloured pens, which will still allow you to capture the beauty of the painting. You may also add some natural materials if you like.

The Navajo follow strict measurements when creating the sand painting. Their exact rules are unknown, so you will have to use your intuition to create a mandala of balance and harmony.

You will need

- Pair of compasses
- Pencil
- Ruler
- Large sheet of paper
- Coloured pens or paints
- Natural materials, such as rice, leaves, stones and grasses

1 Begin by marking out a large circle with a radius of at least 15cm/6in. Draw a line across the centre, then draw a second line crossing it, using the compasses to bisect the 180° angle and establish the perpendicular. This cross in the circle forms the basic medicine wheel, with the four primary directions, east, south, west and north. Mark the mid-point between two directions and repeat this around the circle. You can now draw in the other four directions.

2 Replace the compass point in the centre and draw a small circle at the centre of the mandala, surrounded by a second one to represent the cosmic lake. Follow your instincts when deciding on the diameter of this circle. Now draw a large outer circle inside the circumference, again following your instincts as to how large you feel this needs to be. This circle represents the boundary of the earth, at the point where it meets the sky.

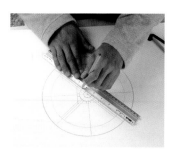

3 Draw a square a small distance outside the central circle and separate from it. Draw parallel lines close to either side of each of the four secondary directions. Draw short lines the same width apart to connect the inside of the square to the circle at each one of the primary four directions.

4 Rule a line across each corner of the square to join the intersections of the two parallel lines, creaing four small triangles. Using the same dimensions draw three more triangles along each direction towards the outer edge of the mandala. These represent the clouds of the sky which bring rain.

5 At the top of this line of small triangles draw a small circle with its centre on the direction line. Rule two perpendicular lines across the small circle to create a miniature medicine wheel. Repeat this small circle on all four secondary directions. These are the four mountains of the Navajo world.

6 Draw two guidelines down the centre of the mandala, the width of the inner circle apart. In the north, begin from the centre point of the square edge and draw a line to the intersection of one guideline with the outer circle. Do the same midway between this and the direction line and repeat on the other side so that you have a fan shape to represent tobacco. Repeat the process in the south to create the squash plant.

7 Draw in guidelines the width of the inner circle in the west direction. Starting from the centre of the square on that side, draw a zigzag line to the top to mark the bean plant. Finally, add leaves to the plant in the east, representing corn and three corn fruits. Tobacco and squash have their fruit on the circumference of the outer circle. The beans hang down from the leaves in the west and corn grows upwards in the east.

8 Finally, open the mandala in the east by removing a section of the circumference. You may want to invite some spirits or good thoughts to come into the centre of the mandala as you do so. The Navajo believe that only positive spirits may enter from the east direction. Draw a stylized head of the rainbow goddess at one end of the opening and a stylized body at the other end. The mandala is now ready to be coloured.

Colours and Symbols

Traditionally the Navajo use only living materials such as cornmeal, crushed flowers and pollen to create the Blessingway, so you may want to use grains such as rice or oats, or leaves, or stones, to build on the symbol of life. For colours the Navajo use one for each of the four directions: white for dawn in the east, blue for midday in the south, yellow for twilight in the west and black for night in the north.

As you paint the Blessingway mandala remember that it is a celebration of life and the precious and unique person that you are. The basic shapes of the mandala represent the unchanging elements of the natural world. The outer circle is the rainbow goddess who surrounds the universe. The cosmic lake is that from which all life emerged and whence it can be purified and reborn. Its boundary with the earth is represented by the square in the middle of the mandala. The small triangles and circles on the secondary directions stand for clouds and mountains, and the four crops, which are all sacred to the Navajo.

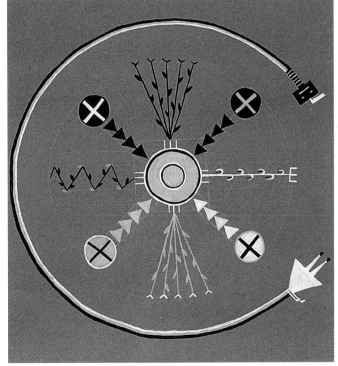

To fill the sand painting you can use paints, inks or any coloured natural materials.

creating new mandalas

There are many different ways to create interesting mandalas that you can put in special places to remind you of your connection with the world and its beauty. The drawing of a mandala can be a spontaneous act of expression from your inner self. However, first it is important to spend a few moments focusing on the part of yourself which you want to get in touch with and bring to the surface.

Using coloured paper can add an extra element of expression.

Drawing an Inner Mandala

First gather the materials you will need. Having a large pad of paper and pastels or crayons handy will save time when the moment to draw comes upon you. Other materials that are very expressive are watercolours, oil paints, and charcoal as these can allow soft and messy feelings to be drawn effectively.

Next, find a quiet place to be alone in peace for a while. Sit down in front of your paper and materials and use compasses or a plate to draw the outline of a circle in the centre of your paper. Close your eyes for a moment. Sit with your back straight and breathe slowly. Try not to think of anything in particular. When thoughts come to you don't follow them but just let them fade away. Count ten slow breaths and let your mind come to rest.

Now in your mind's eye imagine the circle you have drawn. Imagine what shapes you could fill it with and the colours you would choose. Open your eyes, pick up your brush or pencil. Allow yourself to put the pencil wherever you feel is the right spot on the paper. Pick up paints or pencils on a whim and draw whatever comes to mind. Remember that you can change the speed and pressure with which you move your hand. You can do anything, even tear holes in the paper.

As patterns begin to emerge you may find that you want to add layers of colours. Feel free to use your hands and parts of your body to smudge, imprint and outline shapes in the circle. Other parts of you may want to speak as much as your hands. Fill the circle completely. Remember that whatever you do it is right: there is no wrong inner mandala.

Medicine Wheel Picture

Another way to get at your deeper emotions is to create a medicine wheel or Celtic cross picture. Take a large piece of paper and draw a circle. Focus on the circle and use thick water-based paints to spread colour across the mandala. Use colours and shapes that express your feelings at that moment. Now fold the paper in half through the centre and press the two halves together firmly. Push the paint down and move it around inside the folded paper. Pull the two sides of the paper apart and then fold it again through the centre, making the second fold perpendicular to the last one to form a cross. Press down on the mandala wherever you feel the need. When you feel it is ready, open up the paper to reveal the circle of the mandala and the cross patterns and colours within it.

Living Mandalas

Using materials that sustain life can be very significant. Dried simple foods, such as rice grains, oats, seeds, lentils, beans, pasta and flour can all be added to a circle to create complex textured shapes. Find somewhere flat and smooth to work. Use chalk or a soft pencil to mark out the circle and any patterns or guidelines you want to express. Working from the centre of the circle outwards, pour in or place the food materials. Think about the depth of the patterns and the textures and shapes of the ingredients. For example, pasta shapes could be made into a spiral pattern, or oats could be piled into symbolic clouds and mountains.

Use candlelight and incense to create a relaxed atmosphere.

Rose Window

To bring a little illumination into your life you can create a translucent rose window using coloured tissue paper. Select three or four colours that you like and that mix attractively when you hold them up to the light together.

You will need

- Tissue paper in several colours
- Sheet of coloured paper
- Pair of compasses
- Pencil
- Scissors
- Glue stick (optional)
- Coloured thread and needle (optional)

A circle cut from a sheet of thicker, dark-coloured paper makes a frame for the window.

1 Start by cutting out identical-sized circles from coloured tissue papers and from a single sheet of thick paper. Fold the paper circle in half and in half again, Do this twice more until you have a thin folded segment. Now cut out patterns along all the edges, especially at the centre. The most effective patterns come from being bold and yet simple.

2 Put one circle of tissue paper aside: this will be left uncut to form the background to the design. Fold and cut the other pieces of tissue as before, making any shapes you want. Now unfold the paper and tissue circles. Each will be a different mandala, however, you can now layer them together to create the rose window.

3 Use the paper circle as the top layer to act as a mask and frame the different coloured patterns, then layer the tissue circles below it. Place the final uncut tissue circle at the bottom. To bind the layers together you can either use a very small amount of glue around the edges, or sew them with coloured thread at points around the circle.

Sand Mandala

The Navajo Indians have many mandalas, each of which is healing and relates to a highly symbolic myth. The medicine man would choose a mandala appropriate to the sick person's illness. The patient would sit inside the mandala and be healed by the spirits evoked by the mandala.

By using your own instinct, you can design, or choose a mandala that will help relieve you of your worries or ailment. The simple act of creation is itself very healing and the power of the mandala should not be underestimated. Centre yourself as well as you can with a short meditative routine and begin.

1 Use a pencil to draw a simple pattern on a white sheet of paper. Include shapes that are easy to fill with sand of different colours. Pour a small amount of coloured sand on to one area of your pattern. Start with the smaller and lighter areas.

2 Spread the sand around with your fingers until the picture is finished. Next, blow or brush the sand away to leave the paper clean again with all but your initial pencil drawing. Your mandala practice has now been completed.

afterword

The mandala traditions of the Buddhists provide us with a wealth of imagery and symbolism – beautiful circles containing palaces and diamonds, guardian spirits, and lotus leaves. However, the essence of the mandala is translated into every language and culture in sand paintings, medicine wheels, rose windows, stone circles and equations of lines that form computer art. Regardless of time or place, every human being holds at their centre the key to unlock their own unique path to happiness.

The Beauty of Mandalas

Mandalas exist all around us, whether it's in the splendour of the dawning sun or the twisting turns of a winding river. Each image gives another glimpse of the peace that can be found when we are living at the centre of ourselves. Each one is an opportunity to learn how to move to that centre and how to live in harmony with the world. We can all be happy and live the life of our dreams if we choose. There is a universal web of life with which we can fall into harmony and live in peace.

A tree is a living mandala. Each ring of a tree trunk tells a story about each year of its life.

A personal mandala is a symbol of our own unique dream. It can take us from the hustle and bustle of the mundane world with its worries and anxieties to a place where we take responsibility for our thoughts, words and deeds. It can enable us to walk in dignity to the centre of our life, where we long to be. The journey is not easy. In any mandala there are circles of fire to be crossed and tombs of old hurts to be unearthed and laid to rest. At the heart of each mandala, however, lies the centre, drawing us on and waiting for us to reach it.

Beautiful mandalas exist under the sea. The spiral shell of a mollusc grows steadily outwards as it ages.

As the Buddhists say,

See all beings as buddhas;
Hear all sounds as mantras;
Know all reality as mandala.

Speak your truth and live the life
of your dreams.

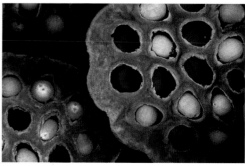

The seeds of a new life form at the centre of a husk. Meaningful patterns are all around us.

templates

Use these templates as guides for making your own mandalas. The easiest way to do this is to enlarge them on a photocopier. If you don't have access to one, you can trace the design and draw a grid of evenly spaced squares over your tracing. Draw a larger grid on to another piece of paper and copy the outline square by square. Draw over the lines to make sure they are continuous. Whichever way you choose, before you begin make sure you are calm, prepared and will remain undisturbed as you express your inner self through the mandala.

Index

Picture Acknowledgments:
The publishers would like to thank the
following libraries for giving their kind
permission to reproduce the pictures
listed below:
A–Z Botanical Collection Ltd: 105T;
119T; 154; 158T.
**Ancient Art & Architecture
Collection Ltd:** 114B.
The Art Archive: 104T; 104B; 155T.
Axiom: 155B.
Bridgeman Art Library: 149R; 156;
157; 158B; 166.
Fine Art Photographic Library Ltd:
119B.
Fortean Picture Library: 154B.
Images Colour Library: 117B; 121T;
123T; 153B; 204TR; 204R; 204C.
Oxford Scientific Films: 160; 161B;
163T; 163B.
Science Photo Library: 159T.
Skyscan: 148T.
Stock Market: 159; 157; 164.
Tibet Images: 150 & 157; 151.
Tony Stone Images: 105B; 107T; 109T;
114T; 121B; 122BL; 122BR.
Werner Forman Archive: 165.